More Praise for *Getting Change Right*

"In this terrific book, Seth Kahan shows that to foster true employee engagement, conversations and human interactions are a lot more valuable than fat budgets and formal authority. *Getting Change Right* is a practical, hands-on guide for managers and organizations interested in making bold changes."
—Daniel H. Pink, author, *A Whole New Mind* and *Drive*

"Trying to drive change within an organization can be a frustrating experience. Human beings are wired for repetition and so find comfort in the status quo. But change is mandatory—in order to compete we must create—and in order to create we must lead the change. Seth Kahan lays out the principles of 'getting change right' and provides practical advice and insight with relevant examples. This book couldn't be more timely!"
—David Kord Murray, author, *Borrowing Brilliance*

"Change is a constant and is accelerating at what sometimes seems to be an almost alarming pace. Seth Kahan has provided practical, down-to-earth advice with examples to help leaders execute a change strategy that will result in employee buy-in and positive organizational outcomes."
—John H. Graham IV CAE, president and CEO, ASAE & The Center for Association Leadership

GETTING CHANGE RIGHT

GETTING CHANGE RIGHT

HOW LEADERS TRANSFORM ORGANIZATIONS
FROM THE INSIDE OUT

Seth Kahan

Foreword by Bill George

JOSSEY-BASS
A Wiley Imprint
www.josseybass.com

Published by Jossey-Bass
A Wiley Imprint
989 Market Street, San Francisco, CA 94103-1741—www.josseybass.com

Jossey-Bass books and products are available through most bookstores. To contact Jossey-Bass directly call our Customer Care Department within the U.S. at 800-956-7739, outside the U.S. at 317-572-3986, or fax 317-572-4002.

Portions of this book are taken from posts that appeared in "Leading Change," the author's column at fastcompany.com, and are copyright © Mansueto Ventures, LLC.

Jossey-Bass also publishes its books in a variety of electronic formats. Some content that appears in print may not be available in electronic books.

Library of Congress Cataloging-in-Publication Data

Kahan, Seth.
  Getting change right : how leaders transform organizations from the inside out / Seth Kahan ; foreword by Bill George. —1st ed.
    p. cm.
  Includes bibliographical references and index.
  ISBN 978-0-470-55048-9 (cloth)
  1. Organizational change. 2. Leadership. I. Title.
  HD58.8.K34 2010
  658.4′06—dc22

                                                                        2009051937

Printed in the United States of America
FIRST EDITION

HB Printing   10 9 8 7 6 5 4 3 2 1

Contents

List of Figures

For visionaries of all kinds: I hope these tools will make it possible for you to see your ideas come to life

Foreword

Bill George

"There is nothing wrong with change, if it is in the right direction."

So said Winston Churchill as he helped guide the Allies through the mire of World War II. Has there been another period since when we found ourselves in greater need of political and business leaders who can heed these words?

Our country's leaders stare down a dismantled financial system and continue to step over the ruins of once-great institutions like Lehman Brothers and General Motors, now bankrupt. To act according to Churchill's adage and "get change right," a new generation of leaders must step forward and possess not only an understanding of the areas where change is necessary, but a concept of what form that change must assume.

In my career, I've witnessed firsthand different ways that leaders (myself included) attempted to steer their organizations and people through difficult changes. Whether it was the introduction of an innovative new product line or an attempted alteration of entrenched corporate culture, the challenge came not in pinpointing the areas for improvement, but in understanding precisely how to enact lasting solutions to achieve the best end result.

Sometimes we got it right, and sometimes we didn't. In *Getting Change Right*, Seth Kahan has developed a series of principles and insights for today's leaders as they navigate difficult changes in their organizations.

At a time when our country's leaders need guidance on enacting change—from a long-overdue cull of rewarding short-term practices on Wall Street to a dismantling of the partisan stalemate on Capitol Hill—Seth has emerged with a beacon for today's leaders and their teams. For everyone from CEOs to mom-and-pop operators, change will come, and Kahan's insights can help them prepare for its arrival.

As a former CEO, I find a great deal of value in Seth's approach. By pairing precise step-by-step guidelines with firsthand accounts and academic insights, he has created a no-nonsense reference for first-time leaders and veteran managers alike. What I found most helpful is the book's accuracy around dealing with the variable personalities you'll find in a given company. In every lesson, Seth takes into consideration the human elements—the egos, the intricacies of teamwork, and the true spurs for personal motivation—that make or break any corporate undertaking, let alone monumental change.

Calling on expertise and insight honed by years of top-tier management consulting and thought leadership, Seth writes with warm savvy and a rare technical expertise that informs leaders on how they can strategically and logistically enact change the first time around.

Leaders who desire to enact effective, lasting change must be prepared for long-term dedication to their company, and Seth demonstrates how leaders can do so with their values, and leadership teams, intact. I've explored authentic leadership values throughout my career and devoted my teaching career to helping future leaders at Harvard Business School develop a concept of "true north," an internal compass of our beliefs, values, and principles that guide us through life. From his thoughts on "Energizing Your Most Valuable Players" to "Breaking Through Logjams," Seth's writing conveys the words and insight of a man who has seen authentic leadership in action.

Seth not only calls on his own vast academic and professional leadership experience, but enlists the firsthand perspectives and anecdotes of other leadership authorities as well. He has amassed a comprehensive guide on change leadership in accordance with one of his own major precepts: enlisting the insights of others to create rapid, widespread engagement. Seth Kahan is a writer who puts his money where his mouth is.

Want to know how to improve your organization's flexibility and responsiveness? Refer to the six pieces of advice Seth gives on that very subject, which are applicable across any organization or team. Want to know how to find and inspire talented team members? Turn to Chapter Three for a step-by-step guide on how leaders can challenge and motivate top performers to a desired end.

In my career, I've discovered that crises offer the prime opportunity for leaders to enact the change they want to see. It is imperative that leaders today recognize the need for institutional change while remaining undaunted by its inevitability. The sailing may not always be smooth, but it will be forward motion. The best leaders know that is sometimes the best they can hope for. And that's what Seth aptly teaches us all in *Getting Change Right*. In the final chapter, Seth explores what he calls WorkLifeSuccess, a concept that speaks to the necessity of balance across work life and home life to achieve success in both.

I would not have been nearly as successful or content across my career without my support network of family and friends or the work-life balance I eventually achieved. Values-driven, perspective-enriched leadership does not occur automatically; I believe it is possible only once a leader establishes the sort of balance Seth advocates. Authentic leaders who are capable of getting change right the first time establish equilibrium between the important facets of their work and home lives, as Seth makes clear in his conclusion.

This, I believe, is the crux of *Getting Change Right*. When striving to enact needed changes in a responsible and decisive way, get the passion, get the know-how, and work diligently to find the right balance for your company and its stakeholders. Thanks, Seth, for a refreshing lesson in change leadership—and good luck to all of you on your changes ahead.

Introduction

Between 1995 and 1997 I participated in two distinctly different change initiatives at the World Bank, both called Knowledge Management. The first one never took off.

The second one changed the organization, and the world, in two short years, demonstrating how a bureaucratic, geographically distributed, multinational, public sector organization can reinvent itself faster than anyone could have planned.

What made the difference in these two initiatives? The short answer is *engagement*. The second initiative took seriously the need to connect to people, listen as much as to share ideas, and involve as many key people as possible in the realization of their goals.

The first knowledge management team I joined was composed of a few select world-class thought leaders who drew on a dedicated budget to design and implement a powerful new tool they hoped would revolutionize the way business was done. We met in closed meetings, witnessed remarkable demonstrations, and marveled at the power of the Internet to spread knowledge.

After a year, I found that very little had been delivered and that the enthusiasm around this initiative was still confined to the original small group and a few others who had recently joined. It seemed to me we were going nowhere, and I made up my mind to end my brief tenure with this group.

I was staying late one evening, writing my letter of resignation, when Steve Denning, a World Bank senior staff member, stopped by and asked what I was doing. Steve was working on a parallel initiative, looking at knowledge from a human-centered view in which technology is an enabler rather than the main event. I told him I was resigning. He asked me to give him an hour before I turned in my resignation.

Later that evening, I had a new job, on loan to the team at the World Bank that Steve led. His group, in contrast to the one I had just left, had no funding and no resources except for a half-time assistant. I joined one other staff member, who was also on loan to Steve from the CIO's office.

Two years later, our little team had grown to six people and spawned over 120 communities to champion our program. Thousands of people were deeply involved not only inside but also outside the World Bank, pushing the Knowledge Management agenda forward on multiple fronts in a giant social network.

Steve worked with bits and pieces and cobbled together resources. But we did much more with the bits and pieces than the first team had accomplished with a dedicated budget.

Whether we knew it or not, we understood what engagement was and how to use it. Our working style was the polar opposite of the first team. We told everybody what we were up to. In fact, we spent a good deal of time in the beginning figuring out how to tell as many people as we could, as fast as possible. We even met regularly with our detractors because sometimes we needed their input the most. The dialogue flowed like a river and often penetrated parts of the organization our team had not formally reached.

Within two years, we had achieved international prominence, receiving recognition from independent evaluation organizations and regular visits from business gurus. Our program obtained $60 million in annual allocations. More than that, we influenced hundreds of lending projects, with an impact on perhaps millions of lives.

Seven Lessons for Getting Change Right

In retrospect the second team did a lot right—by intuition and accident as well as by design. We also made a lot of mistakes. From my involvement with these two very different knowledge management teams, I identified seven important lessons, which I still use in my work leading world-class organizations through major change:

1. Communicate so people get it and spread it.

The "it" is not a precooked, hard-boiled message. Instead, it is a conversation that spreads, a dialogue that arouses passion and creates its own social network. We learned to spark cascades of conversations.

2. Energize your most valuable players.

People are at the heart of change. We always took the time to engage. We went after people and gave them exciting ways to be part of the action.

3. Understand the territory of change.

Every organization has a different culture and different ways of figuring out how to go forward. I systematically listened to others to create a map of the change territory.

4. Accelerate change through communities that perform.

We called our communities *thematic groups*. They were essentially groups of people who shared passion for a particular topic and put their passion into practice. These groups advanced our cause, creating systemic pull.

5. Generate dramatic surges in progress.

Special face-to-face events accelerated our program. We created gatherings that brought players together in high-value, high-leverage experiences designed to push things forward in leaps and bounds. For example, as one of our first events, we brought everyone in the organization together who was already an evangelist or who had a strong personal stake in our success. Sixty attended, some of whom were none too friendly toward each other. At the end of our session, we had created a sense of joint ownership among almost all who attended, and our small team had become the de facto owners of the initiative.

6. Break through logjams.

Obstacles, hurdles, and challenges are all part of a change initiative. We had a SWAT team mentality: we expected trouble. We did not see difficulty as a hindrance to our success. Rather it was unavoidable, and in fact, it made many valuable contributions to our overall achievement.

7. WorkLifeSuccess to sustain high performance in the midst of change.

Because success in work is integrally connected to success in all aspects of life, I use the term *WorkLifeSuccess.* By this, I mean doing what it takes to achieve and sustain overall excellence. Things happened so fast it was sometimes disorienting. Our small team used each other and people in other organizations engaged in similar initiatives to keep our focus. Our success in work was drawn from our successes outside work, and vice versa.

As a practitioner, I have written this book for other practitioners. Since 2002 I have worked for over thirty organizations, including Shell Exploration and Production Company, Ernst & Young, NASA, Peace Corps, World Bank, International Bridge Tunnel and Turnpike

Association, Project Management Institute, Johns Hopkins University Applied Physics Laboratory, and the American Nurses Credentialing Center. The techniques I present are based on real-life experience leading change hand-in-hand with CEOs, executive directors, and senior managers of these world-class organizations.

I wrote this book for practical visionaries—people with their eyes on the horizon and their feet on the ground, professionals with real work on the line. It is not filled with suppositions and hypotheses. It is filled with techniques and methods that work and stories that recount direct experience.

It is for managers who are working to implement new and better ways of working in challenging situations where the variables are not always in their favor.

It is for leaders inciting movements consisting of people with real concerns and real questions.

It is for people everywhere whose job it is to make the world a better place and yet are faced with turmoil, ambiguity, and conflicting forces that batter them, making work difficult at best.

I hope that you will apply these methods, procedures, strategies, and tactics and succeed. That is why I wrote them down.

Imagine what it would be like if you could have the rapid, widespread impact of the second World Bank team. What if your great idea could spread far and wide, improving the ways we work and the results we achieve? Imagine that, and let me help you make it real.

GETTING CHANGE RIGHT

Creating Rapid Widespread Engagement

L et's cut to the chase. Without engagement, you won't have buy-in. You are left with two alternatives: force and failure. There are occasions when force works. This book is not about failure.

Force works when it is okay if people don't care. Or if they think you are wrong, giving bad, misguided, or rotten direction, and they're willing to do what you say because it doesn't affect them, is not detrimental in the long run, or the consequences of not doing what you say are more than they can bear.

In all of these situations, people will act on your ideas only so long as someone else keeps them in front of their nose. This is called the *lighthouse effect*. Wherever the change leader casts her attention, it is as if a light is projected, and the people inside that light spring into action, visibly demonstrating how they are enthusiastically carrying out their mandate. But just outside the light, activity quickly slips back into chaos.

This is typical of new ideas. It happens because their importance, significance, and value are not shared. Instead they are imposed. Shared value takes place when people get together to construct the meaning of a new idea or application. Imposed value happens when one person or one group sends an idea out—as if all that is required is that others understand their intentions.

This does not work for two reasons. First, people are overloaded with demands and barrages of information as well as multiple, conflicting mandates from above whose purpose they don't understand. Second, even if you can get their attention (and you will with the techniques I show you), this way of communicating by commands and directives—*"Let me tell you a better way," "I have the answer; the information, knowledge, and research . . ." "I have been giving it good thought and consulted with the experts and we have figured it out"*—is built on the wrong communication model.

I am going to show you a better one, one that works in the tumult of modern organizational life. This way of thinking about communication forms the core from which everything else in this book emanates.

In 1996 I was working on my first large-scale change initiative at the World Bank. I was part of the small team that won international recognition for the World Bank's Knowledge Management (KM) effort. Working on this program was like driving on a racetrack that was changing its course while you steer: the course and the environment were always changing, but we made incredible progress.

In two years we went from an unfunded idea in a back room to $60 million in annual allocations, from no resources or incentives to every staff member receiving two weeks to dedicate to KM as well as having a component of their annual evaluation dedicated to it, from no recognition to international awards.

To make this happen we had to answer questions like these:

- How do you penetrate the conflicting demands and mental clutter that are part of everyday business life in the twenty-first century?
- How do you penetrate the assorted messages the media constantly bombard everyone with?
- After you have gotten through this confusion, how do you get people's attention?
- Once you have their attention, what do you do with it to get people engaged, involved, and contributing?

- How do you coordinate this activity when you have no formal authority?

To answer these questions, let's first look at the prevailing misunderstanding of how communication works, and then I will show you a much better way to think about it.

Most people intuitively use a communication model that originated in 1948 and was published by Shannon and Weaver in 1962.[1] Although this model was great fuel for the information revolution, it is completely inadequate when it comes to person-to-person meaning making—which is what drives the rapid spread of new ideas.

In its own domain, the Shannon-Weaver model is extraordinarily useful and can be credited with initiating much of modern information theory. It has been called by some the "mother of all models."[2] It states that you have an *information source* that develops a *message* that is sent using a *transmitter*. The *signal* travels and encounters *noise* on its way to a *receiver* where the subsequent *message* is delivered to a *destination*. (For a visual depiction, see Figure 1.1.)

The unquestioned assumptions that percolate in the minds of a typical communication team betray their use of this model. They go something like this:

We will talk to our president [*Information Source*] and craft a message that is easy for people to understand [*Message 1*]. We will place this message in various media including newsletters, posters, e-mails, Web sites, and town halls [*Transmitters*]. If we can get people to stop and read what we wrote, take the time to attend our events and listen to what we say, they will be exposed to our concepts and ideas [*Signal*]. Although they are uninformed, distracted and overloaded [*Noise*], they will hopefully read our writing when it appears in their inbox, come to our events, and listen to our presentations [*Receivers*]. They will then interpret what they have read and heard (Message 2) and understand what we are about. We will have reached them [*Destination*].

FIGURE 1.1 Shannon and Weaver's Communication Model

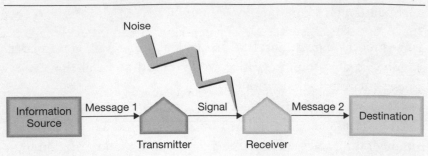

Although the Shannon-Weaver model is great for sending digital signals, it is horrible for people trying to make sense of their world. We thinking humans are just not as simple as this model.

Making meaning is a much more complex task. For example, we don't just decode information and understand it. If we did, you could pick up any book in a university library, read it cover to cover, and fully absorb what the author intends. But you cannot. You also need teachers and other students.

The reason we need teachers and other students is that we construct meaning socially, through interactions. We need the input of others to help us develop our ideas, place them in context, and make them relevant to our world, our experience. It is a collective project. This is called *social construction*.

We construct our understanding of the world through our relationships. As human beings we thrive on liaisons and partnerships. Social construction gets to the heart of how people make meaning together. It opens possibilities for reaching people who understand the world very differently, creating collaboration among diverse participants.

It is also a humane way of looking at communication, enabling compassion and kindness. Importantly it makes it possible to extend these qualities to technical and business-oriented interactions, bringing people together and generating esprit de corps even when people are from widely differing cultures. This is a critical milestone in communication.

Here is how social construction works. One person makes a statement of some kind, putting an idea out for the other to respond. Then there's a reaction, an answer of some kind, which probably includes new information. For example, some part of the original idea makes sense and there's an acknowledgment. Or some aspect appears wrong and there is a negative response or a correction. Or maybe it's not clear yet, so there is a request for more information.

And so the participants go along together, making moves and countermoves, building a shared understanding or not being understood. Either way, an experience is generated that becomes a touch point for future interactions. And so together, back and forth, in messy iteration, understanding is fashioned.

Here's an example:

Raj: Hi, Juanita, I have this new direction from our boss, Sylvan. He says I have to ask everyone for input before we plan our next conference. He isn't sure we did such a good job last year of checking with everyone to see if their needs were being met as far as the agenda goes. He wants to me to ask you what you thought of last year's conference.

Juanita: Last year's conference was a disaster. But it wasn't because Sylvan didn't ask for input. As I remember, we had a lot of input. It was because he took us to the beach in the monsoon season. Nobody wants to go to the beach then! He should have taken us to an indoor resort that time of year or scheduled a time when the beach would be fun.

Raj: Okay, so you had the chance to contribute to the agenda, and the content wasn't a problem; it was the location and time of year. Is that right?

Juanita: Yes, that's right. But now that I am thinking about it, what is the process for putting together our agenda? Are you just going to ask everyone and then put together a hodgepodge of whatever people tell you?

Raj: No, we're going to meet with Sylvan and do our best to outline what we think we should cover. At the same time, I'm going to talk with everyone and ask them what I'm asking you. Then we're going to compare what we hear with what we put together on our own. At the end, Sylvan will look at everything and make some decisions.

Juanita: So we're just going to do what he wants to do regardless?

Raj: I hope we can influence him with the results of these conversations. I think he's pretty open to what we have to say. I don't think he's a tyrant.

Juanita: If anyone can influence Sylvan, it's you, Raj. He loves the way you think. But I'd be surprised if he doesn't dictate the agenda in the long run.

And so the conversation goes, to and fro, each one putting forth a proposition or question and the other reacting, refining, then putting forth a view until the conversation comes to an end. It's not that a consensus is reached, but that Raj and Juanita have both developed and refined their sense of what's meaningful through the interaction.

How does this apply to communicating new ideas and getting widespread engagement? Becoming adept in this kind of back-and-forth construction is where the value is. It is not in the technical smarts or the ability to articulate your own position. Those certainly play important roles, and any good idea is doomed without them. But the real challenge is in high-quality interaction, because that is where people decide if your message is relevant or worth their time and attention, and subsequently develop their sense of how best to act on it.

Here's the kicker: professional expertise abounds. Technical know-how is in great supply. This is referred to as *hard skill.* But engagement, participation, and the genuine desire to contribute rely on goodwill, a cooperative attitude, sincere interest, and a desire to be helpful. In most change programs, these are in short supply. This is the *soft stuff.* In today's work world, the soft stuff is the hard stuff.

This book is about getting the soft stuff right. This is the people part of change. You know the systems will work, but the people may not. And people can corrupt a perfectly good system. With the wrong attitude, they can let obstacles go untended, ignore necessary protocols, and turn their gaze away from difficult challenges. But when they share feelings of pride, a common loyalty, and fellowship, they will create synergies, become inspired to address difficult challenges, and unite in their efforts. This is what makes change happen fast.

Social Construction in a Nutshell

Social construction is a way of looking at how people build a common understanding and negotiate their way into the future. Here are five core principles:

1. *The ways we come to understand the world and ourselves are created in relationships.* All of our understandings spring from our interactions with others. During our lives, we develop a history of relationships—a set of traditions that come from the groups we belong to (family, professionals, jobs, and others). From this springs the ways we think about our experience and the world, including what we believe to be real, fair, and good.

2. *We do not all interpret the world in the same way.* Two people who observe the same event may come to different conclusions. This is normal. What is obvious to one person is not necessarily obvious to another.

3. *Our shared interpretations of the world survive only if they are useful to us as individuals.* If you want me to change my behavior, get involved in your idea, and take on the challenges it presents, then show me what difference it makes in *my* world and why I should care. Make it easy for me to see why I would get involved. Make it clear exactly how I can take action. Show me a spreadsheet that has no impact in my day-to-day life or ask me to read a report that does not change what I know or do, and there will be no additional shared understanding as a result.

4. *Our understandings influence the ways we behave and possibilities for our future.* For example, if we belong to a group that regularly recounts how powerless we are to influence a management decision, we will likely do little to sway it for better or worse. However, if we think we have strong influence, we are much more likely to become engaged.

5. *Reflection on our assumptions—what we take for granted—is vital to improving performance.* Because our view of the world is something we construct, we have the ability to change it with reflection. To maintain our self-determination, our capacity to adapt and influence, we must continuously call into question what we take for granted. This happens by listening to others who see the world differently and wrestling with the consequences of their perspectives.

Social construction is a way of thinking about how people develop their beliefs about and understanding of the world. It provides critical insights as to how people from differing backgrounds navigate their way forward together.

At the center of every good working relationship is shared understanding. Social construction puts tools in our hands to guide the development of this understanding. Most important, it shows us that different perspectives are as legitimate and valuable as they are common. It provides helpful guidance for bringing people together to build common understanding. This is fundamental to getting change right, creating engagement across different communities with different ways of understanding the world.

Moreover, if we look closely, we see that each person is different—even the two guys in the boiler room who work next to each other five days a week or two office workers who work together and think together on the same problems eight hours a day every workday. Though they are side by side, each has a different and legitimate viewpoint. If you want to engage them, and the thousands of others who will bring your change to life, you must give them something to do, draw them into conversation, accept their experience and stories, and allow them to change yours.

Social construction does a great job of explaining how people create meaning together, influence each other, and generate a way forward. Using this as your communication model, you can do a much better job of reaching people and working together to create, communicate, and spread innovation.

KEN AND MARY GERGEN ON SOCIAL CONSTRUCTION AND LEADING CHANGE

Expert Input

Ken and Mary Gergen are recognized thought leaders in the field of social construction. Ken teaches at Swarthmore College and Mary at Penn State University. They are also active in the organization they helped found, the Taos Institute (www.taosinstitue.net). Ken calls the institute "a group of scholars and practitioners exploring the idea that through our relationships we construct our realities and futures together."

This husband-and-wife team works in tandem, developing ideas, writing, convening thinkers and practitioners, and promoting social construction.[3]

Ken: Our society places great emphasis on the individual, including when it comes to leading change. We place a single person, a champion if you will, at the center of all activity, as if a lone person could be responsible for introducing new ideas and driving them to fruition. In the constructionist view, the emphasis on the individual is replaced by relationships. Our views of the world are formulated within relationships, jointly created. The implication is that no one person is the originator of an idea. At base, all ideas are created through interactions.

Mary: That's not to say that there isn't room for people to shine through, for their presence and influence to be felt. Each person draws on many experiences, a history of relationships, to inform the meaning they make of the world. And when they interact with others, they bring all these points of view with them. This takes the whole idea of persons as coherent in their views and attitudes and stands it on its head. If you look at communicating to advance a new way of doing things, social construction is going to tell you to open up the conversation, to bring more people to the table.

So when you are leading change, dialogue with many different groups is important?

Expert Input

Ken: Often we have a conversation in one relationship, and we expect it to apply across the board. But every interaction circulates assumptions that are locally shared. These ideas don't always translate to other relationships. They can even unintentionally suppress or dampen other ways of looking at things.

How do you compensate for this?

Mary: You have to open a space in which people who have radically different ways of looking at the world can contribute. Encourage people who might otherwise be marginalized to give their perspective.

Ken: Every interaction generates meaning unique to its context. Effective leaders have to develop their abilities to include diverse people and span these different contexts. In this way creativity is also stimulated.

THREE THINGS CRITICAL TO CHANGE LEADERS

1. *Reaching people.* To make contact with people, you must success-fully penetrate the ongoing onslaught of information and competing demands from others.
2. *Responding to changing needs.* To be responsive, you must get feedback, pull in relevant information to flex and adapt to emerging conditions as they develop.
3. *Spreading innovation.* To extend new ideas and better ways of working so they catch hold, you have to involve others in building the future.

Penetrating Information Overload

People are pulled in so many directions as to be rendered ineffective at much of what they do. Everyone is pushing forty initiatives forward an inch, and no one is pushing anything forward a mile except you. You have a mission to accomplish So how do you get through the mountain of mandates, responsibilities, and irrelevant information?

You do it by building an initiative that helps the people who will bring your initiative to life. I call them your Most Valuable Players (MVPs). (For explicit detail on who exactly qualifies as one of your MVPs, see Chapter Three.)

You work together to construct paths forward into the future that resolve the dilemmas both you and they are facing, bring aid and support to their most difficult challenges as well as your own, and create wins both of you can take to the bank. When supporting your initiative becomes the best way for others to resolve their most important conflicts, ease the pressures that daunt them, and help them get ahead in ways they care deeply about, they will see you as an ally. That's when they will join forces and begin to work for your success because it is interwoven with their own.

All of your efforts on this must be genuine. If it is a charade or a sales job, the veneer will crack, and your effort will backfire. You will have new enemies, and your initiative will suffer untold harm. But if you genuinely weave your stakeholders' interests into your common future, you will become a master of the win-win, and the results will be amazing.

FIVE WAYS TO PENETRATE INFORMATION OVERLOAD

1. *Call a special meeting to address your stakeholders' concerns.* Bring in the people who matter most: their boss, critical partners, peers of influence, thought leaders in their field, customers, and members.
2. *Bring in your most valuable players to evaluate a critical decision you are facing.* Make a thorough presentation that lays out the context, the options, and the dilemmas. Ask them to think both independently and together about the best way forward. Highlight win-wins as they appear. Take action based on their advice, and give them credit for their guidance.
3. *Do something countercultural to catch attention.* Take on the concerns and issues of those who show resistance and make them

your cause célèbre, attracting public attention and support. This is an effective way to reverse hostility and join forces with those who would oppose you.

4. *Stage a concentrated series of highly visible activities.* In a very short period of time, appear to be everywhere at once. Contact your constituents during this campaign and ask them to help with the design, planning, presentation, or execution of your project. Give careful consideration to their contributions, incorporating what you can.

5. *Go directly to the source of competing demands to win support.* For example, call a meeting of all managers who supervise the people you want to engage and demonstrate the effectiveness of their subordinates. Connect their common self-interest to the objectives of your initiative.

Effective change leaders master the art of cutting through the daily bombardment, piercing the chaos, and replacing it with opportunities to succeed.

This accomplishes success on two levels: (1) the way you work enrolls more and more people, creating the network and momentum for continued success, and (2) you are more connected with day-to-day life, enabling the greater flexibility and responsiveness which keeps your effort relevant and on track.

Establishing Flexibility and Responsiveness

It is essential to become adept at listening to and integrating new knowledge into your program as news breaks and circumstances change. When you establish a program that is tightly connected to current events, able to receive and integrate important changes as they occur, you secure two important things necessary for dramatic success.

First, your reputation will precede you, bringing people to your side even before you open your mouth. Interested parties—those looking to improve things themselves—recognize the power of a program that is adapting to the winds of change, adjusting appropriately as situational factors shift.

Second, you will build in the necessary feedback mechanisms for real success. As you will see over and again in the pages ahead, you and your team have a limited perspective. Yet you serve in critical roles: champion, herald, coordinator, convener, context creator, strategist, designer, inspirer, executor, momentum generator, communicator, harvester, and broker.

You are cultivating a multidimensional response from a complex system, and feedback is fundamental to your success. Your effort is multidimensional because it operates in many spheres of activity, some of which act independent of others. You must have your finger on several pulses simultaneously to steer through successfully.

Because you are operating in a complex system, it is not always clear what actions influence what results. In a linear system, if you push, you see the impact. In a complex system, this does not necessarily happen. The impact may be so removed in time that you cannot observe it directly. Or the push may be part of a system that causes its impact to be amplified, diminished, or even ineffective. In this situation, you rely on the eyes, ears, and minds of others to provide the necessary guidance.

As a single person or a group, you have by definition limited access to the entire system. Therefore, your perspective and your understanding will constantly be tested, stretched, expanded, and enhanced by others. This is one of the most valuable and most difficult challenges of successful, large-scale change.

SIX TECHNIQUES FOR IMPROVING FLEXIBILITY AND RESPONSIVENESS

1. *Know the core intention of your work.* For example, the core intention of a program in a large government think-tank was to bring the best minds to bear on the most important challenges. It was not to build a fully searchable document storage tool or create professional

communities. Those were tactics. As the political environment changed, the tactics changed, but the core intention held firm. Holding onto the core intention allowed those working on the program to take constant pushback and maintain progress continually.

2. *Intentionally invite people who hold opposing or adjacent views to be thinking partners.* Import other perspectives. Purposefully embrace the challenge of looking at your own initiative from other points of view.

3. *Embrace new ways of looking at your work that are difficult to understand.* Sidestep the temptation to see one perspective as right or dominant. Instead, allow the tension to resolve in ways that do not compromise either view. This takes time and patience. Having a tolerance for this kind of work leads to much more robust solutions.

4. *Understand the assumptions that you bring to your efforts.* Is there any player who is diminished as a consequence of your perspective? If so, meet with him to learn about and build respect for his experience. This is one of the most difficult activities you can engage in, but it is also one of the most powerful. It will broaden your understanding and increase the strength of your work.

5. *Create mechanisms that encourage or incentivize others who see things differently to provide constructive ideas.* An example is an anonymous e-mail inbox that allows people to comment on the success of the program. Periodically publish comments that you have taken to heart and acted on.

6. *Ensure that news travels transparently through your office, without censure.* Set an example of successful media coordination, providing others with relevant reports, communications, or articles that might aid their success.

Creating a Shared Stake in Success

Success at leading change—dramatic, sustained improvement—is largely determined by a leader's capacity to not only enroll others but engage them in a mutually supported vision of the future. *Engagement* means getting their whole-hearted support and participation, their involvement and best actions. When this is happens, change is held in place by myriad hands, heads, and hearts.

Achieving a shared stake is critical because obstacles are part of life, and you need all the help you can get to realize success. You want resources to flow to you—people, money, and time to be dedicated by any and all who see a shared road to success. When this happens, synergies will take place you do not mandate or coordinate. You may not even be aware of them because the ideas have successfully spread, and other people in other places are taking action.

FIVE TECHNIQUES FOR CREATING A SHARED STAKE IN SUCCESS

1. *Practice exceeding others' expectations.* Every morning ask yourself how can you "wow" somebody who is critical to your success. Then meet with her face-to-face to express your appreciation and discuss how your combined efforts are creating a better future. Ask, "What synergies do you see in our work?" Listen and learn.

2. *Engage others in conversation* to discover their answers to these questions:

    a. What are your most pressing issues?
    b. What needs do you have that are not being met?
    c. What successes are you working toward?
    d. Who are your constituencies, and what do they want?

    Then explore with them how these can be addressed through your efforts.

3. *Hold meetings with groups of allied players to identify mutual goals.* Follow up with regular progress reports showing the results of your efforts and the challenges you encounter. Work together to overcome obstacles and clear logjams.

4. *Create a visible representation of your key players' interpretations of success.* Post it where others can see it easily. Do not require different or conflicting views to be reconciled. Instead, invite people to view

the representation with you and think together on how seemingly irreconcilable objectives could be achieved. This generates a sense of inclusion among all who participate and mutual ownership as everyone sees their thumbprints on the future.

5. *Ask senior stakeholders to describe in detail the future state they are working toward.* Go through the details with them and listen carefully:

   a. What does this future state look like? Describe it in detail. What will be different? What new capacity will emerge?

   b. How will you know it when it happens? What are the indicators you will look for? How will success be measured?

   c. What are the benefits to you personally? To the organization? What is the return on investment for the effort?

   Write up what you learn in a one-page summary and present it back to each senior member you interview, or otherwise visibly demonstrate what he or she communicated to you. Verify with them that you have captured their point of view. If necessary, refine it with their input until they are satisfied.

Laying the Groundwork to a Shared Future

The only way to have a new idea catch fire is to set it free in the world in ways that enable as many people as possible to begin using it constructively. That's when exponential growth occurs.

Interaction lays the groundwork of the future. You must get out of your office and talk to people. Find out what they are facing and learn how they see the world independent of your needs and goals.

We are constantly generating the future through interaction with unforeseen events and circumstances. The understandings we carry— what we are doing, where we are going, what and whom we are hoping to influence—shape our responses and initiatives and our behavior.

Communication, done well, enables us to (1) make sense of what is going on around us, (2) decide where to put our efforts, (3) balance the needs of the moment with our long-term goals, and (4) take action.

Communication done poorly does the opposite: it (1) confuses us, (2) makes it difficult for us to choose where to put our effort, (3) distracts us from the needs of the moment and our long-term intentions, and (4) stifles effective action.

Once you begin using communication effectively, you will immediately win support of a very important contingent: those who are focused on getting things done well, resolving pressing circumstances, and moving steadily toward their overarching objectives. This is the first layer of effective penetration. Simply by doing a good job of communicating, you attract others who are effective because they rely on a social network of effective communicators and you have joined them.

The implications are significant. For example, it means you can't just send a well-crafted memo (or report or PowerPoint or spreadsheet or presentation) and expect people to read it and change their behavior to conform to your conclusions. And yet that is essentially what most communication efforts amount to.

Think about it for a moment. A report consists of words on paper. Without people to read and interpret, reports are just sheets of paper or bits of magnetized metal. All the action is in the interpretation of the people who wrestle through the document and absorb it into their relationships where they make sense of it and take action with others. Social construction tells us that this process needs to happen with other people, not in the privacy of a single brain.

This is why getting people together, face-to-face, to share air, is so important. Today we have lots of technology that makes it possible for people to talk otherwise—everything from telephones and chatrooms to state-of-the-art videoconferencing facilities. But face-to-face is still the most valuable, highest-leverage activity.

So what's a change leader to do? Create ways for people to get together and converse. Get them participating, engaged, and involved. This is the road to personal investment, enthusiastic support, and genuine buy-in. This is how you move people across the line from "I *have* to do this" to "I *want* to do this." And that makes all the difference in the world.

Getting people involved in thinking together about new ideas is difficult for many leaders. Often they think they have to invent the universe in advance or at least figure out all the major components. But social construction shifts the emphasis away from "let's figure everything out in advance" to "let's do a good job of starting the conversation and get the right people involved."

To succeed, you become an ace at bringing people together and creating healthy interaction. How to do this is the focus of this book.

It's the difference between you or your office pushing all the information and having a network of change agents pushing *and* pulling from multiple points simultaneously. If it's up to you to do all the pushing, then everything slows down or stalls when you stop. When you have a distributed network of change agents in action, they create synergies and drive the program from multiple points simultaneously. This results in more effective widespread engagement.

GETTING CHANGE RIGHT

Getting change right means:

- Bringing people together and helping them interact in ways that create meaningful engagement for new and better ways of working.
- Tapping into a high-leverage web of experience and information so your initiative responds in real time to changing circumstances.
- Getting many, many people on board as quickly as possible, creating a fast-paced buy-in.

When people grab your ideas and run with them, you will find the increase in speed and reach growing faster than you can keep up with it! This is a good thing. It means your change is taking off. This is how success happens.

Eight Conversations That Create the Future

For each of the eight conversations that follow, you must establish an atmosphere of genuine exploration. These topics are meant to open the doors of perception to new possibilities, creating an environment where half-baked ideas can emerge for examination and development, insights can form, and new possibilities can edge their way into view.

Think of each topic as one variation on a theme, and come back to it over and again in the conversation from different angles. In this way, you can generate a series of questions and adventures, each revealing possibilities for how you might go forward together.

The Eight Conversations

1. What is the best possible thing that can happen as a result of our efforts?

    a. What performance improvement is possible as a result?

    b. What could this mean to you, me, and us?

2. How do new ideas successfully take root in our culture?

    a. Where has success happened in the past?

    b. What innovations have we operationalized with good results before?

3. Where do the trajectories of our efforts converge?

    a. What are the possible synergies if we are both successful?

    b. How can we leverage each other's results?

4. What motivates us to succeed?

    a. What is the source of our inspiration or motivation?

    b. How can this be leveraged for even greater returns?

5. What would be the consequences if we were both successful?

    a. Can we describe this world?

    b. How would individual and organizational work be improved?

6. If we were to generate dramatic results, what partnerships would we rely on?

   a. Who else must we involve in our achievements?

   b. How do we provide returns to them?

7. What prerequisites do we both rely on to achieve big wins?

   a. What can we do to ensure we have what we need?

   b. Where can we combine efforts to ensure success?

8. How can our interdependence be improved?

   a. What are the opportunities for mutual leverage?

   b. Where can we exceed expectations by working together?

Accelerating the Speed of Buy-In

Value is at the heart of all negotiations. Your job as a change leader is to enter the worlds of your stakeholders, learn what they value, and find ways for your idea to help them achieve that as quickly as possible.

There was a period in my work when I was called in over and over again by a large bank to help teams that had become stifled or stuck and watched their productivity take a nosedive. It was difficult work. Often my first engagements were with groups whose animosity was high and I was there to create a breakthrough.

One group had taken on a particularly visible project that the CEO was watching closely. The team was made up of two groups: the technology specialists, or *techies,* as they were known to their peers in that company, and the content specialists who were called *SMEs,* for subject matter experts. They were working on delivering a series of solutions over the Internet to people in many countries around the world. The whole idea was to take the SMEs' knowledge and deliver it straight to the client, through the Web.

The CEO was hopeful that this would create a breakthrough in delivery, and the CIO (chief information officer) was keen to demonstrate his ability to generate solutions to the company's challenges. So all eyes were on this team. The team, however, had completely broken down after six months. The techies had what they considered to be great solutions but felt the SMEs were inept when it came to technology. So they were reluctant to show them anything but a finished product. The SMEs resented the condescension and wanted to be involved throughout the process.

The SMEs were guilty of the same judgment, but in their area of expertise. They were sure the techies had no idea about the content and were unable to provide real content for the techies to work with, thinking it would be misrepresented and the company would be liable for resulting catastrophes.

By the time I arrived, all communication had fallen apart. I walked into a silent room with eighteen professionals sitting at desks, looking down at their notes or glaring at each other. No words at all. Before arriving, I had read all of their materials. I have a strong background in information technology, so I was able to grasp enough of what the techies were up to so that I could have an intelligent conversation with them, though the details were beyond me. And the SMEs had provided me with a thorough detailing of their material.

I sat down in the silent room and waited a minute before speaking. Because the quiet was so heavy, it seemed to concentrate the moment.

"Why are you here?" I began, and then continued: "Let me tell you why I am here. Then I would like to know from each of you why you are here." I said, "I am here because I care about this organization. I want to see it succeed. I was brought in because this is an especially important project, and the powers that be want you to succeed. Let me tell you just a little more about myself."

I had spent the morning with my son and was carrying a picture of him with me. Spontaneously, I pulled out the picture and showed it. "This is Gabriel," I said. "I am here because I want the world to be ready for him, and I am committed to doing what it takes to give my best to make that happen."

I passed around the picture of Gabriel and went on. "Part of my job is to make sure we do our very best everywhere we have an opportunity to make an impact, and this project has the potential to make a great impact. I want you to succeed, I want him to succeed, and I want to succeed. That's why I am here. Why are you here?"

Then I shut up. There was a long moment of silence. Eventually the lead SME spoke up and said that she was there for a different reason: she wanted to use her professional training to make a positive impact in the world.

Slowly we went around the room and heard from everyone. There were several themes as to why folks were in the room. Nobody else mentioned his or her children, and I was a little uncomfortable that I had said something that had maybe not been well received. However, it became clear that my vulnerability unleashed a much-needed conversation about people's personal motivations for the project. The overriding theme from the team was that they were there to offer their professional expertise, knowledge, and experience that each had paid a significant price for. This was their moment.

When everyone had spoken, there was another silence. I was tempted to break it, but I let it last instead. Finally, the lead techie stood up and spoke: "We are in the midst of rapid prototyping. We need to move through our iterations quickly. We have been hesitant to let you [he pointed at the SMEs] become involved because we have concerns that you will slow us down. If you will work with us to do this at a good speed, I would like to invite you to join us in the process."

That broke the ice.

My job was over. The team went on to deliver a great project and even named themselves the *Collaboration Community*.

It took only forty-five minutes.

During that one meeting, everyone put their cards on the table— why they were there. For most of them, there was value in demonstrating their professionalism to the CEO, the CIO, the organization, their peers, and each other. For some, it was different. But a way forward was found that gave each what they were looking for.

Once it became apparent how to generate value for each person on the team, there was more than agreement. There was committed action.

That is buy-in. From that moment on, each person invested personally in the success of the team, and their results were stellar.

The lesson here is one that has come to me over and over again, and it permeates this book. There is no shortage of professional talent in the world. Superlative efforts result when we are able to create a shared spirit of joint success. Then nothing can stop us. Oh, and by the way, *this takes only a moment.* Then it's all for one and one for all. That's the heavy lifting.

THIRTEEN TECHNIQUES FOR ACCELERATING BUY-IN

1. *Create a team of change agents.* Teach your most avid supporters, your evangelists, how to listen and have productive conversations with everyone they meet. Regularly conduct role plays where they bring in their toughest situations and learn from each other how to handle them well.

2. *Replicate your team.* Teach your evangelists how to teach others to have these same productive conversations.

3. *Adapt and integrate your ideas with multiple contexts.* Those much-touted elevator speeches (rehearsed speeches that can be delivered in the time it takes for an elevator to reach its destination) are almost useless for most great ideas because they are disconnected from context and make no sense to many listeners. Practice connecting your ideas to different contexts by raising it in different circumstances.

4. *Distribute easy-to-understand teaching tools.* Provide anyone who wants to advocate on your behalf with the materials they need to explain your ideas and their benefits. Use the materials yourself. Set an example.

5. *Leverage strategic reflection.* Create time to review what is working, what is not, and how you can change your behavior to increase the speed of change.

6. *Build a web of thinking partners.* Find people who understand what you are trying to do and have the professional experience and expertise to help you develop your activities.
7. *Become expert in efficient and effective communication.* Use media tools that disseminate relevant news immediately to all parties.
8. *Choose a network over a hub-and-spoke relationship model.* Make it easy for your supporters to reach each other without going through you. Provide everyone with e-mail addresses, telephone numbers, and access to project tools — anything and everything that allows them to initiate collaboration on their own.
9. *Delegate everything — or as much as possible.* If you have a budget, pretend you don't. Move activities and responsibility out to the periphery so it can spread.
10. *Follow enthusiasm and commitment.* Go where the energy and excitement are. Make time for people who are dedicated and supportive. Blow their coals into fire.
11. *Provide as much face time as possible.* If you use electronic media, turn to them to enable people to get together. Whenever possible, share air.
12. *Create time in your day to talk to others.* Don't become so overloaded with tasks that you can't have a conversation. Remember that dialogue is the basic building block of change.
13. *Dedicate space for conversation.* If possible, have a living room or somewhere else with a casual atmosphere where people can congregate when the need arises. If all you have are conference rooms, make sure that everyone knows they are available for casual conversations and impromptu meetings.

Why Formal Authority and Budget Don't Matter

Solid, lasting change is not about answering to authority. It is about real application that makes good sense in the many levels that people have to operate in every day. This kind of change can catch and spread through a system faster than any one person or group can dictate, and that's a good thing.

For the same reason, it has little to do with budget. Now, I would never turn down money. If you offered me a budget, I would tell you in short order that I can spend it. It's just that I have seen good ideas take off like wildfire with no money behind them. A perfect example of this is the second KM change initiative I participated in at the World Bank.

As I mentioned previously, in 1995 I was recruited to join the team building the World Bank's Knowledge Management System (KMS). It was a small team with a dedicated budget whose mission was to design and implement a powerful new tool they hoped would revolutionize the way business was done. We had the unwavering support of the CIO. He regularly spent time with our project manager. We paid for some of the best minds in the industry to come and work on our KMS. We were told that we had permission to change the way the Bank did business. We had the authority to design a revolution.

One year later, the enthusiasm was still confined to a small group, and it seemed to me we weren't progressing. That was when I made up my mind to leave and Steve Denning approached me with a new job. In contrast to the first group, Steve had no money or resources. He also did not have much recognition for his program. He had landed in the IT department because the Bank did not really have any other place to stash him.

Steve had been on the rise in the Bank's Africa group. Just as he neared the top of that organization, the president of the World Bank, Lewis Preston, died. Shortly afterward the Bank was reorganized, and Steve was given the job of dealing with information overload. As Steve tells it, this was the equivalent of being sent to Siberia.

Steve was a guest in the IT group, working with virtually nothing. Yet in the next two years, our little group did way more than the first team ever accomplished with a dedicated budget. In fact, we did more than teams that had millions of dollars in their budgets. Whether we knew it or not, we intuitively understood what engagement was, and we set about doing it.

Two years later, our team had expanded to a grand total of six people and achieved the phenomenal results I wrote about in the Introduction. We had also developed a network that included over 120 communities inside the organization to champion our program. Thousands of people were deeply involved both inside and outside the World Bank, pushing the agenda forward on multiple fronts in a giant social network. And we started this all without formal authority or budget.

We identified all the people who were major players and contacted them regularly. We convened those who understood and supported what we were up to—our evangelists. We met with directors and project managers who had the most to gain from our ideas. We brought in key players like the World Bank publisher, whose participation could make or break some of our most important efforts. And we didn't stop there.

We invited *anyone* who was interested to be part of our work.

We created working groups. We met with clients. We visited other agencies that were doing what we were trying to do and brought them in to visit us. We met with business thought leaders like Peter Senge. We even met regularly with detractors.

We met with everyone, everywhere, at every opportunity. We lived in a river of conversations that never stopped. The dialogue spread and flowed to parts unimagined and permeated the tiniest crevices, until everything was wet with new ideas and innovation. Everywhere we went, people were thinking about Knowledge Management—what it meant to them and their work, how they could become involved, and the benefits it could bring to their beneficiaries.

The power of the transformation was awesome, even unnerving. It traveled so fast and far that it often outreached where our little team was able to go.

STEVE DENNING ON OPERATING WITHOUT BUDGET OR AUTHORITY

Expert Input

Steve Denning is the global thought leader on organizational storytelling. He has written five books on the subject, including two award-winning books: *The Secret Language of Leadership* and *The*

Leader's Guide to Storytelling.[4] The *Financial Times* chose *The Secret Language of Leadership* as one of the best business books of 2007, writing, "If business leaders do not immediately grasp the vital insights offered by this book, both they and their organizations are doomed."[5]

Steve is the former program director of knowledge management at the World Bank, where he spearheaded the organizational knowledge-sharing program. When I served on his team, I had the chance to work hand-in-hand with him leading a large-scale change initiative.

In November 2000, Denning was selected as one of the world's ten Most Admired Knowledge Leaders by the Teleos Leadership Institute.

When I joined your team at the World Bank, we had no real authority to speak of. Clearly this did not stop you from pressing forward. What can you say about leading without formal authority?
Well, formal authority can be a real problem. We did get the support of the president, Jim Wolfensohn, and that was helpful. He furnished us with a clear message: "We will become the Knowledge Bank." But it was just as important to our success that we did not have middle management breathing down our necks. What you want is someone outside the team giving clear priorities—"Here's the goal," "Here's the vision"—and then a tear in the fabric of the universe. Space opens up that allows the team to self-organize into high performance.

What about budget? You started out with no money.
It was a blessing in disguise. When you're given budget, you have to figure out what to do with it, and other people try and take it away from you. It creates a whole set of distractions that take your eyes off the real work, which is talking with people and discovering together what's possible. Of course, we needed resources. But they came as we needed them. When I needed more people, you and Lesley Shneier, a senior knowledge and learning specialist, were given to me on loan. When we needed to put on an event, like the Knowledge Fair, we made it enticing enough that people paid to be a part of it.

So the resources came as real value was generated. When there was something worth pursuing, people showed up and helped to fund it. It was all based on real work. Most initiatives are based on someone's idea of what should happen. They ask for money first, and then they have to figure out what to do with it. If they spend it on their idea and nothing happens, they look bad. We didn't have to worry about that.

We created activities and events that people looked at and said, "I want to be involved in that. I'll pay to have a table in the fair; I'll let the group meet in my conference room; I'll host that event."

Principles for Creating Rapid, Widespread Change

The World Bank's Knowledge Management Program delivered results around the world for years. Many of its initiatives survive today in various forms despite changes in leadership, budget slashing, staff turnover, and reorganizations.

I have used four guiding principles since that powerful World Bank initiative with every organization that seeks my services:

1. *A great idea in the hands of champions trumps formal authority any day.* Unfortunately, formal authority is mostly associated with bureaucratic requirements or top-down mandates rather than enthusiastic engagement. Champions, in contrast, take on ideas because they have confidence and vision. Followers detect the difference easily.
2. *A great idea implemented through engagement takes on its own momentum and generates the funding it needs to succeed.* As success mounts, people are able to recognize ROI and invest accordingly.
3. *Groups of enthusiastic, competent professionals develop applications, ideas, and innovations that go beyond anything one team can dream up.* We were constantly amazed by the power and far-reaching implications of the KM efforts. It went far and away beyond our expectations.
4. *Engagement takes ideas further, wider, and faster than any one group can control.*

I have discovered time and again that widespread esprit de corps is far more effective than having power in the hands of a privileged few in terms of speed, reach, and effectiveness. It's that simple.

Success Rules

- Getting people on board requires a new, deeper understanding of how people communicate and create meaning together, and lays the groundwork for the future. Social construction provides this.
- Getting change right is about:
  - Penetrating information overload and competing demands
  - Establishing flexibility and responsiveness
  - Building the shared future that creates buy-in and engagement
- Conversations create the future, so you have to get out and interact with your most valuable players.
- Getting people to participate and invest in your initiative is about generating value they can take to the bank.
- Success can be achieved without formal authority or budget.

Communicating
So People Get It
and Spread It

A chain reaction is a string of interactions, each of which creates a by-product that starts another reaction. When the number of reactions grows exponentially, you get a cascade as one reaction begets two, and each of these begets two more, and so on.

In 1933 Hungarian physicist Leó Szilárd moved to London to avoid Nazi persecution. There he learned about the awesome nature of atomic power. He had a history-altering insight, theorizing that an atomic chain reaction was possible if he could find an element that would release two neutrons when bombarded by one. He foresaw that this would release amazing amounts of energy.

His theory was correct. He found the element, uranium, while doing research at Columbia University with Enrico Fermi. Szilárd later participated in the Manhattan Project. His work made it possible for U.S. scientists to create the nuclear chain reaction that lead to the atomic bomb. Amazing amounts of energy, indeed.

Just so, when you create an interaction that then generates other interactions, you produce amazing impact. As one person talks to two and two talk to four, the number of conversations grows exponentially, creating powerful increases in the speed and spread of change.

When I say, "Communicate so people get *it* and spread *it*," *it* is not a concept that moves through the system until it has infiltrated everyone's thinking and changed their behavior. Yet this is precisely what most people try to engineer. *It* is instead a conversation that travels through the population, an interaction. Each conversation generates more conversations, exciting others with possibilities, enrolling them in the cause, lighting the way to contribute, and inspiring action.

If you want your idea to spread, you need to become expert in these areas:

- *Leading conversations that engage.* These are interactions that weave people into your work, making them collaborators, co-creators of a shared future.
- *Generating cascades of activity.* Set off chain reactions of meetings and conversations that are carried from those who experience you firsthand out into their social networks.
- *Conducting strategic engagement.* Here you are like the conductor of an orchestra, only you are coordinating events instead of music. You adjust the timing, create emphasis, highlight virtuosos, provide critical feedback, and create a balanced effort that is cohesive, compelling, and powerful.

This chapter shows you how to do all three.

FIVE CONSEQUENCES
OF SUCCESSFUL ENGAGEMENT

---

1. *Your message goes fast and far,* creating traction, involvement, participation, and buy-in.
2. *You generate goodwill.* People spend less time in a reactive mode, judging your efforts, and more time pitching in, telling you what they think and helping to create solutions.
3. *People perceive that you understand their needs, perspectives, and potential.* They see genuine evidence of their success in yours, and you do the same. It is a reciprocal relationship.

4. *You weave the results of your change effort into the social fabric,* connecting it to the events and unpredictable circumstances of everyday life. In this way, it becomes practical and integrated, gaining traction and growth as events unfold.
5. *You achieve sustainability.* The myriad brains, hearts, and hands that support your program operationalize new ways of working and create a web of support that is difficult to undo.

Getting change right is less about producing communiqués and more about cultivating relationships. This is a true paradigm switch—from a model in which you design and assemble messages to one in which you till, plant, nurture, weed, and harvest affinities. This is a living model rather than a mechanical one.

Elevator Speeches Only Take You Down

One of the fundamental problems in communicating change is quite simply that most professionals don't know how to hold an engaging conversation, much less teach their supporters how to do the same. The traditional approach is to take a great idea and turn it into a slogan, an elevator speech, and a campaign. This amounts to one-way communication and sabotages engagement. There may be discussions, town hall meetings, and coffee chats, but unless you're spending more time listening than you are talking, you're creating three results that are taking you backward instead of forward.

First, you are generating bad press for your change. Every person who doesn't see the world the same way you do (in other words, almost everyone else) is thinking quietly while listening to you drone on: *This person has no idea what my life is like.* When they walk away from the conversation, they have pegged you and your program. Not what you want.

Second, by precooking your idea, you are stepping free of reality— the constantly changing, swirling, messy, and upsetting chaos that makes up day-to-day life. Your change idea becomes an ideal, isolated from the real world and devoid of traction and growth.

Third, you are ensuring that you or your office, the keepers of the message, are the primary source of change. You are thereby limiting your impact and sealing your doom.

This is hard to swallow for those who believe they can succeed by simply mapping out a project and then executing it. Real change is about growing a successful reception and including many players in the dreaming and the realization of new ways of working.

Project Planning Can Be a Costly Diversion

The biggest drain on momentum and brainpower in change efforts today is obsession with the project plan. I have seen more projects flounder and die because leaders and consultants are hammering out finely detailed project plans rather than engaging people.

As my friend Larry Forster, staff engineer at Shell Exploration and Production Company, says, "The good news about a project plan is that you get what you plan for. The bad news is that is all you get."

I asked Larry what he meant by that and he explained: "Project planning is a good and necessary aspect of leading change. But if you stick too close to it, there are many wins you won't realize because they are not programmed in. The biggest risk is the support of the people who you have to have on board to make change stick. Project plans don't usually have an allowance for enthusiasm or fortunate synchronicities. Yet these are some of the most powerful enablers of long-term success."

People create project plans for many reasons. Here are three I see often:

- *It is tempting to imagine how you will create change.* The downside is that people get sidetracked into imagining it rather than doing it.
- *It is challenging to engage people.* This requires good interpersonal skills and a willingness to repeatedly open up messy conversations. Many technical experts prefer to avoid this and instead work solo or with a small group of like-minded colleagues, on dependencies, resources, and time lines.

- *People often confuse building a mental model with the real thing.* They think, *The more we work on our plan, the more we are getting done.* Until the rubber hits the road, you have accomplished *nothing.*

It's true that a project plan is useful and even necessary in most situations. It's a question of appropriate emphasis. When I am after change, I want to make things happen—get results, reap rewards. This happens through people, interactions, networks of conversations, and people working together.

Project planning is a support process. Engagement is the main event. It's where people shift attitudes and behavior. You do not want the project planning to occur at the expense of engagement, replace conversation, delay interactions, or exclude participation. But the obsession with project planning is a difficult habit to break. It's so much easier than to go out and start another conversation with someone important, someone you respect, who has never heard about what you are doing and will ask a lot of fundamental questions when you don't really have the answers. Yet that is exactly what's needed. You need to become expert at getting people involved in co-creating the future, jump-starting bold conversations that draw people in, and triggering professional excitement.

Leading Conversations That Engage

In 2006 I was called into Shell Exploration and Production Company by Larry Forster to revitalize the adoption of a new technology. Enthusiasm was on the wane, and the merit of the benefits of the technology was cloudy. It wasn't clear to the people who worked and supported the rigs in the Gulf of Mexico that the new technology would be helpful to them. They were not sure it was worth the overhead required to install and use it.

Our goal was to bring everyone together to renew and reenergize adoption. This meant we had to clearly identify the value of the new technology. Then we could do three important things: (1) confirm the commitment to adopt the technology on one specific asset (an asset is an oil well or gas field), (2) generate new interest for other assets where the value was clear, and (3) discard adoption on any assets where the value could not be justified. In essence, we wanted to get on with adoption where it was the right thing to do and cease adoption efforts everywhere else.

But first we had to engage all the important players—everyone whose expertise was needed to make a good decision. This included representatives from headquarters in Rijswijk, the Netherlands; managers of several of the assets; engineers who worked on the assets; and technology specialists. The problem was that they were all in various states of support, ranging from out-and-out enthusiasm to apathy, concern, and even animosity toward some aspect of the adoption.

After we identified the critical stakeholders, I contacted each and began to engage them in our effort. As a neutral party, I was a critical part of this first contact. I had served in this way for many years as an employee, so I know it is not necessary to go outside for this expertise. However, it is absolutely critical that first contact is made by listening and learning, not propagating an agenda.

These are the three steps to initiating contact that I always use:

1. My sponsor sends everyone an e-mail introducing me as a neutral party and requesting fifteen to thirty minutes of their time to fill me in on the situation.

2. I make contact with each, arranging a time to speak. I never send a mass e-mail. This is the beginning of a relationship that I will leverage throughout work together. It should be personal.

3. Once in contact on the phone or face-to-face, I introduce myself, tell the person our goal is to do the right thing with the new initiative, and then ask if he or she sees the situation. While listening, I do my best to understand the other person's point of view. I ask questions to clarify his or her perspective and often repeat back what I hear, actively listening to grasp this person's point of view.

I take notes during the interviews, including quotes. Later I review them with my sponsor and write up a Reconnaissance Report in which I identify themes in the interview conversations and provide unattributed quotes as supporting evidence. (For more on this and a sample report, see Chapter Four.)

The situation at Shell was complex. There were cultural conflicts, disagreements over needs and value, varying levels of support, lack of information on the technical details, and the unique circumstances of each asset and each person involved. A simple solution was not apparent. Nonetheless, in a few days, we were able to engage twenty people in an exercise to revitalize adoption of the technology.

EIGHT PRINCIPLES FOR ENGAGING NEW STAKEHOLDERS

1. *Introduce yourself as a neutral party.* This gives them permission to tell their unadulterated point of view.
2. *State that the call will be confidential.* This opens the door for information that might otherwise be filtered out, facilitating greater disclosure.
3. *Say you want to do the right thing.* This is a value-neutral statement that can be interpreted positively regardless of the other person's views. It helps instill a constructive tone to the interaction.
4. *Ask the stakeholder to provide her experience.* This solicits her story provides a wealth of material and building rapport.
5. *Put yourself in her shoes.* You want to really see the situation through her eyes. Reflect back her words to ensure you comprehend what she is telling you. Suspend your own views as best you can to be open to her ways of understanding the circumstances as distinct from you own. This allows you to explore her values, hopes, aspirations, and needs.
6. *Interpret what the right thing to do is from her point of view.* Offer it for inspection, amendment, and correction, and hone in on it until

you have captured her perspective. Understanding how she believes is best to move forward from this point increases your rapport.

7. *Express appreciation for her professional judgment and time.* Letting her know that you value her offering begins a relationship of reciprocity.

8. *Invite her to join you in finding a good way forward.* This show that you respect her professional viewpoint and sentiments. It establishes a way for her to reciprocate and exert influence over what may become an important event.

Everything is designed to effectively weave new stakeholders into the way forward with the adoption revitalization. By listening to their stories, opinions, experience, know-how, and judgments while returning to the point that you want to do the right thing, you create traction, involvement, engagement, and buy-in because your work is perceived to be relevant, attuned to, and successfully addressing the concerns of the people you are seeking to engage.

With the revitalization effort at Shell, we made sure that we were addressing the concerns of the people we were working with. We started by listening to them and their concerns. We were able to get close enough to seeing it through their eyes that we constructed a meeting built on their wants and needs regarding the new technology.

The event was a success, freeing up energy in the organization for the new technology. Decisions were made. Enthusiasm was roused. Value was reestablished. Implementation was either reconfirmed or cut short because it was seen as lacking the necessary justification. (The details on how we created this breakthrough are laid out in Chapter Seven.)

Jump-Starting Bold Conversations

There are many ways to get people involved. You can have a conversation with them, talk to their boss, force an issue that will have an impact on them, and so on. I focus on the voluntary aspect of engagement for two reasons.

First, the most powerful kind of participation is that which generates enthusiasm and spreads of its own accord. This relies on people choosing to talk and then follow up with some kind of action. At the core, with or without a mandate, voluntary involvement is ultimately necessary.

Second, if you can master this kind of engagement, everything else comes more easily. Once you know how to get someone contributing because he wants to, you can use these same techniques on those who are required to give time, money, or work.

My work since 1989 has primarily engaged economists, technologists, researchers, scientists, accountants, administrators, and engineers. None of these are very far out on the touchy-feely continuum of personality types. Nonetheless, I am able to consistently arouse their enthusiasm, enroll their voluntary participation, secure their buy-in, and generate their contributions by appealing to their professional spirit. I position all of my change work in the context of helping the individuals involved to reach higher levels of professional development and explore the frontiers of their expertise.

The best work raises the bar for both individuals and organizational performance, and a project or change initiative should never downgrade one for the other. The following questions are designed to show people that getting involved with change can improve their professional standing by initiating courageous topics that stimulate aspirations and lofty goals. It is one of the best, cleanest, and most inciting techniques I know to generate the interest that leads to engagement.

FIVE QUESTIONS THAT TRIGGER PROFESSIONAL EXCITEMENT

1. What is the best possible outcome of this initiative in terms of your career?
2. What professional breakthroughs can this effort be used to facilitate?
3. What is the highest bar that has been set in your area of expertise, and how can this program help you to exceed it?

4. What is your next step professionally, and how can this work help you get there?
5. What does every professional who shares your role in this company most want to do, and how can we make it happen as part of what we are doing?

TEN QUESTIONS TO ENGAGE OTHERS IN A BETTER FUTURE

1. What is the right thing to do?
2. Given this background, what do you think is the best way to go forward?
3. How can any competing forces be reconciled?
4. What options are there for resolving these conflicts?
5. What are some of the best choices for going forward?
6. Can you name the dilemmas and suggest alternatives for harmonizing them?
7. Given that we don't see eye-to-eye, how can we generate real progress?
8. If circumstances do not change, what is your advice for rectifying the situation?
9. If you could look at this from above, how would you resolve it for all parties?
10. Can you name creative solutions that we have not yet considered?

To master this approach, you have to go beyond seeing communication as a way to get your message out. Instead, your goal is to generate interactions that lay the foundation to a shared and improved future. This is how transformation happens.

FOUR PRINCIPLES FOR CREATING CASCADES OF CONVERSATIONS

1. *Make story your medium.* People don't remember bulleted points, and they don't get excited about them. Stories lodge in our brains and are easy to remember and recite.
2. *Tell your stories everywhere there is interest.* You and your team must make it a priority to travel anywhere there is interest among your stakeholders, tell your stories, and provide access to your materials.
3. *Make support materials easily available.* Anyone who wants to contribute to your cause should have easy access to the latest and greatest materials to support your cause. The Web is the ideal delivery mechanism.
4. *Pursue strategic engagement.* Create a plan for to support your overall goals.

Creating Cascades of Conversations

The goal for rapid, widespread engagement is that the conversation greatly exceeds the reach of those who initiate it. This means that many people in many different places are talking about your effort, and thereby advancing it, without you to supervise or control it.

Let's take a good look at the prerequisites for enabling and inspiring others to pick up your ideas and run with them.

Make Story Your Medium

When I first came to large-scale change in the mid-1990s, I was a storyteller. The World Bank was my day job so I could pay my bills and eat. But my passion was performing folktales and legends.

Grimm's fairy tales, King Arthur and the Knights of the Roundtable, Native American teaching stories, Jewish tales, and original stories were my focus.

I performed for children and adults in a wide variety of settings. When I went to work for Steve Denning, he was searching for a way to get the message out to thousands of World Bank staff who were spread around the globe and of many different nationalities.

After I was transferred to Denning's team, he took the initiative to get to know me. I remember him asking what my hobbies, interests, and passions were. On several occasions Steve watched me perform stories. Then, at a World Bank picnic, in which I did an impromptu performance for a small group of kids, Denning had a powerful insight.[1] He became mightily interested in storytelling, seeing it as a way to propagate ideas throughout the World Bank, around the world.

He gave me the assignment to find storytellers who had experience working in organizations. I called the National Association for the Perpetuation and Preservation of Storytelling (NAPPS) and found only one.[2]

Rick Stone, an independent consultant and founder of the Story-Work Institute, was making a presentation to YMCA staff in Richmond, Virginia, just two weeks later, so I drove down from Washington, D.C., to watch him in action. His message was strong, and his techniques were effective. Stone was, and is, a pioneer in the field, a thought leader, and an expert practitioner.

Steve and I invited him to visit us at the World Bank, and before long, we began a joint venture with NAPPS to run a series of think tanks. Funded by Eastman Chemical Company, they included people from Hewlett-Packard, Lucent Technologies, Ernst & Young, Harvard University, Disney, the World Bank, and others. Stone put the program together and led many of our sessions.

As a result of this exploration, we deepened our understanding of story as one of the most powerful forms of human communication. We learned that different types of stories had different kinds of impact.

Rick Stone on the Power of Story

Rick Stone was the first storyteller I met who was applying the art to organizations. He is a former advertising executive who saw the power of story and started the StoryWork Institute, dedicated to harnessing the impact of storytelling.

Expert Input

When I first got interested in storytelling, I was using it to help people. I developed a program to help parents tell stories to enhance family life. Then I met a chaplain who was working in a hospice and offered to do a program for his staff. It went very well, and soon I was working with hospices around the country.

It was clear that my work moved people, that it stirred something deep and made a difference in their daily lives. But I did not connect it to leadership until a good friend from graduate school told me the work I was doing was applicable to organizations and leadership development.

What was your first business engagement?

I went to a former client who was doing pest control. I approached him and said, "Hey, I have these crazy ideas about storytelling. Do you have a problem in your business where we could try something out?" He said, "Yes, we do!" He had a problem in south Florida with ghost ants. If you don't exterminate them correctly, they split into two or three colonies and spread. His salespeople, who were also providing the service, were under so much sales pressure that they were cutting corners when it came to treating the ghost ants. So they had to go back and retreat often. My client guessed it was costing him about a half-million dollars per year. I did a workshop for his managers, and it was reasonably successful. The whole idea was to use storytelling to create a new set of behaviors that would stress quality and service over sales. It gave me a chance to try something out that was very values oriented in a business environment. When it was over, I knew something was here.

Fast-forward to the mid-1990s when you put together a think tank in Jonesborough, Tennessee, under the auspices of the International Storytelling Center. What was that all about?

Expert Input

We brought people together from many distinguished organizations that were each interested in organizational storytelling. It gave them the chance to talk about their work. In their own way, each person was exploring the power of story in an organizational setting, and it was an opportunity for us all to learn from each other.

The interesting thing is that there was all this good work going on. Disney considers itself a story organization and takes story very seriously in its culture. Harvard's Project Zero focuses on learning and was interested in the power of story to convey information. The World Bank was looking at how to spark massive change in a decentralized, multicultural environment. And so on. There was so much good work being done. The think tanks gave us the opportunity to make it visible and put together people who were energized about applying storytelling. What became clear in a very short period of time was that storytelling fulfills a primal need to gather and tell stories. I like to call it the desire for the *central fire*. It is very powerful.

Denning became most interested in stories that sparked action. His first book documented his experience at the World Bank and discovery of what he coined *the springboard story*—a kind of story that sparks action.[3]

A *springboard story* is a bare-bones and true story that illustrates the change one is trying to create by telling where it has already taken place. It documents the actual time and place, so that your listeners can look it up on their own and verify the change, and it highlights a protagonist—the main character—your listeners can easily identify with.

SIX CHARACTERISTICS
OF A SPRINGBOARD STORY

1. It communicates the specific change you want to initiate.
2. It identifies an incident where the change has already taken place, including time and place.

3. It has a protagonist (main character) your audience can readily identify with.
4. It is stripped of unnecessary detail, that is, it is just the bare bones.
5. It has an authentic, verifiable happy ending.
6. It concludes with an invitation for listeners to imagine what life would be like if this change were to take place.

Let's say you are trying to convince the CEO of your firm, a publishing house, to recruit a more diverse workforce as a way to improve performance. You first go looking for a verifiable success.

Let's say you find one at the First Spring Publishing House (this is a fictitious example) and you tell this story to your CEO at the next senior team meeting:

> In 2005 the CEO of First Spring Publishing House, Martha Siff, made a commitment to improve performance by recruiting a more diverse workforce. Throughout 2006 and 2007, its diversity increased, and in 2008 the company realized a 35 percent growth in sales and a 27 percent increase in productivity. We have not taken these steps, but imagine if we did.

You see right away how short this story is. It is not an exercise in imaginative detail. It gets right to the point, conveying how the change desired had the consequence you are seeking. Stories have the unique ability to be apprehended in ways that bullet points do not and are much more easily recalled.

Harvard's Graduate School of Education runs Project Zero, a research group whose mission is to "understand and enhance learning, thinking and creativity in the arts, as well as humanistic and scientific disciplines, at the individual and institutional levels (http://www.pz.harvard.edu/index.cfm)." During the storytelling think tanks, David Perkins, a codirector of Project Zero at the time, participated. In a conversation, he asked me how many bullet points someone can be expected to remember in a difficult situation? *Three,* I answered. "No," he said. "It is one. Think of that next time you are putting your PowerPoint together."

Stories bundle ideas through associations and thereby make it possible to remember much more and to remember it in context. All your listener has to do is remember one of the ideas, and the others come along for the ride.

When stories are shared, they move from one context to another. In this movement, they provide meaning to the people who are sharing them. This meaning is the life force that spreads and creates excitement as the stories move from one mind to another.

The spread of ideas is about exciting people in a context that is meaningful to them. But there is no way to predict what that context will be. Here is the power of the story. Each well-told story is multifaceted. So stories provide many handles for listeners to grab. Yet the story remains essentially the same. This is what makes it possible, for example, for stories to travel down through the centuries and remain relevant despite widely differing conditions. Think of the Old and New Testaments, the Quran, the story of Buddha. They have crossed eras and continue to hold currency to this day.

I work with stories because they have the capacity to span cultures and still retain context, and therefore also their capacity to inform and influence.

Tell Your Stories Everywhere There Is Interest

You and everyone on your team must become proficient at traveling to other company locations, presenting your material and engaging people in constructive conversations. Going to your stakeholders, rather than requiring them to come to you, is an act of courtesy that initiates reciprocity. By taking the initiative to visit, you win support.

Just after the first Shell workshop to reinvigorate the adoption of new technology, Larry called me and said, "We're going to Rijswijk."

"What are we going to do?" I asked.

"I don't know," Larry said. "We're going to find out what we are going to do. We're leaving in two weeks."

Over the next fourteen days, through a series of phone calls, we established contacts and a host. We told people we were coming to listen and learn. When we arrived, we were greeted as guests. Our schedule had been assembled thoroughly. In each eight-hour day, we had six one-hour appointments and two sessions to reassemble with our hosts, debrief, and share what we were learning.

Relationships blossomed. The connections that we formed were solid and carry us through in our work to this day. In addition to meetings, there were evening beers and long walks late at night, reflecting on everything from the new technology to the meaning of life.

It was one of the best moves we made. We simply showed up, told our story, and listened to theirs. We shared our intentions and aspirations and listened to their points of view, concerns, and issues. They made it clear that the fact that we took the initiative to visit them across the ocean was received as an act of respect and a desire to collaborate.

Many successes were created as a result.

Go out among your stakeholders, tell your story, and provide easy access to your most effective materials.

Make Support Materials Easily Available

Support materials are tools and artifacts. They do not replace interaction. Rather, they accelerate conversations, extend relationships, and make it possible for others to become evangelists. Anyone who wants to provide momentum should have easy access to the latest materials that support your cause. The Web is the ideal delivery mechanism.

Support materials include PowerPoint decks, documents, spreadsheets, videos, audio files, and anything else that conveys what you are doing. If your materials are not widely and readily available, you have greatly constricted your impact. The whole idea of rapid, widespread engagement is that others can speak for your cause. Make it easy for them.

SEVEN WAYS TO DISTRIBUTE
SUPPORT MATERIALS

1. Set up a Web site, and put links to your best materials on the front page in an easy-to-find location.
2. Send out regular e-mails that include links to your materials in the signature.
3. Every time a new product or service becomes available, send out a press release to all known stakeholders.
4. Provide support, and explicitly invite people to use the materials. Tell them you are available to answer any questions that may come up as they download, read through, and make presentations.
5. Carry copies of your placards, posters, and brochures with you. Hand them out. Tell people they should feel free to use them. Put a note on the materials that says, "These materials are available for your use, to serve your needs. Please copy and distribute them freely within your organization."
6. When others create their own materials, call them and praise them heavily. If they got it wrong, offer to help them with the details. *Never* criticize them for well-intended efforts.
7. Send out a packet from the CEO that includes a short (one paragraph is best), personal, signed message encouraging and praising the use of your materials.

Pursue Strategic Engagement

In addition to becoming expert in leading engagements, you must think strategically.

Ronald Heifetz is the King Hussein bin Talal Senior Lecturer in Public Leadership at Harvard University's John F. Kennedy School of Government. For the past twenty years, he has generated critical works that have influenced leadership theory in every domain. Heifetz often draws on the metaphor of the dance floor and the balcony.

Let's say you are dancing in a big ballroom.... Most of your attention focuses on your dance partner, and you reserve whatever is left to make sure you don't collide with dancers close by.... When someone asks you later about the dance, you exclaim, "The band played great, and the place surged with dancers."

But, if you had gone up to the balcony and looked down on the dance floor, you might have seen a very different picture. You would have noticed all sorts of patterns... you might have noticed that when slow music played, only some people danced; when the tempo increased, others stepped onto the floor; and some people never seemed to dance at all.... The dancers all clustered at one end of the floor, as far away from the band as possible.... You might have reported that participation was sporadic, the band played too loud, and you only danced to fast music.

... The only way you can gain both a clearer view of reality and some perspective on the bigger picture is by distancing yourself from the fray....

If you want to affect what is happening, you must return to the dance floor.[4]

So you need to be both among the dancers and up on the balcony. Conducting strategic engagement is a balcony activity. Paired with your activity leading interactions, you have both balcony and dance floor in operation.

TEN RECOMMENDATIONS
FOR STRATEGIC ENGAGEMENT

---

1. *Engage senior management.* Create regular interactions or briefings. Better yet, join the senior management team. Create a position that requires representation at the highest levels of your organization. If that's not possible, put together an executive council. Integrate your program with the overarching objectives of the organization, and be ready to flex as they change.

2. *Bring in professionals who understand the change process.* Find one consultant you trust to act as a personal coach. You need a neutral perspective from an expert who can listen to your point of view and concerns and provide you with one-on-one strategic reflection. This is the single greatest amplifier of productivity, minimizing your downtime and optimizing your impact.

3. *Create an engagement strategy.* Map out a clear business justification of activities, including a time line. The purpose is to clearly convey to leadership and other interested parties what you will be doing and why. Have it ratified by leadership, incorporating their input and resources. An example is given in Appendix A.

4. *Avoid surprising people.* Give advance notice when you are going to provide a keynote or lead a meeting. Do your work in advance to ensure maximum uptake. If concerns arise, respond to them in advance.

5. *Provide impeccable follow-up.* Check back with people following an interaction. Ask them if there is anything you can do to help their efforts. Most will not need direct assistance, but the offer will build your relationship with them. Those who do request help will be leveraging your presence and are worth the investment.

6. *Align yourself with communication, training, and support.* These are the folks who handle the soft stuff, which we know is the hard stuff. Treat these relationships with special care, and work toward full integration.

7. *Create streamlined approval processes within your team.* Make it possible for your group to turn on a dime and respond quickly. This is one of the most effective ways to win support and stay ahead of the game.

8. *Work with multiple media in synchronized releases.* Splashes are described in detail in Chapter Six. The prep work and follow-up required to pull this off are well worth the return in strategic forward movement. (This topic is addressed in detail in Chapter Six.)

9. *Conduct regular surveys to assess your effectiveness.* Never lose contact with your most valuable players. Surveys should be face-to-face whenever possible. I meet regularly with valuable players, and sometimes send teams out with clipboards to have five-minute conversations with many people in a short period of time. Electronic surveys are a distant second to live interaction, but they are useful in many situations.

10. *Do extensive team building with your group and the most valuable players.* In an environment of constant change, having close alliances with as many critical players as possible is a strategic imperative.

SIX GOALS FOR INTERACTIONS WITH OTHERS

1. *Build trust.* This is first. Without it, everything else falls apart. Surprisingly few leaders give it the importance and attention it deserves. First and foremost is to demonstrate graciousness and respect for your audience. Always remember that if you mess this up, they can take you out. You can't do change alone.

2. *Seed the conversation.* Come well prepared with your materials. Introduce only enough to initiate and guide the conversation. This is not a data dump. You are creating an opportunity for others to become engaged. Begin where they need to get on, and stop when you have said enough.

3. *Listen.* This is active listening. Put yourself in their shoes. If you don't understand what they are saying or feeling, ask. Demonstrate your intent to understand. Ask for clarification. I often say, "Can you say more about that?" Then reflect back what you have heard. Prepare for your understanding to be incomplete or wrong. This is not a showstopper; in fact, asking for help to get it right is one of the most effective ways to garner enthusiastic support.

4. *Learn.* Every interaction is your market research, so you can't afford to get it wrong. Go into every conversation to increase your understanding. If it's not happening, take the initiative to make it happen. Find ways for every person or group to become your teachers.

5. *Inspire.* Share your vulnerabilities and enthusiasm. Learn how to express your emotions in your presentations. The word *emotion* comes from the Latin, *movere,* to move. You must move your audiences to action, and emotion is your key.

6. *Connect.* Always provide support materials, tell people how to get in touch with you, and where to find more information.

Interacting with Audiences of Difference Sizes

As you lead engagement activities, you will find yourself in one of five situations:

1. One-to-One: You talk with one other person
2. One-to-a-Few: You talk with a group of two to five others
3. One-to-a-Small-Group: You talk with five to thirty others
4. One-to-a-Large-Group: You talk with thirty to three hundred others.
5. One-to-a-Very-Large-Group: You talk with more than three hundred others, including thousands of people.

There are some important differences to consider for maximum engagement with each of these groups. Nevertheless, your primary objectives in every case are the same.

Each of these five audience sizes is unique. You will move on a continuum from the greatest sensitivity of one-to-one to the greatest boldness of one-to-a-large-group. Here are some brief guidelines that will ensure your success in each situation.

One-to-One
This interaction is clearly the most intimate and also the most nuanced. There is no place to hide. Follow the other person's lead for style of

interaction. Think of the interaction as a dance, and note whether she takes the lead. If she offers you the lead, take it graciously. If instead she takes off, follow along closely.

Try to get as close to her as possible through the interaction without creating discomfort. Aim for a tightly coordinated interaction that takes the best of both of you to create something neither of you could replicate on your own.

One-to-a-Few

You are in an ensemble of two to five others here. Pay attention to the group as a whole. Look for opportunities to take the lead, but don't hold onto the reins unless it is expected.

Think of this interaction as a jazz band. There are standards, traditions of relating, that open opportunities for solos where one person takes the lead for a while. Concentrate as much on the traditions as the openings. In a group of this size, and all those larger, you are outnumbered. To succeed, you must lead as much as listen.

Set the pace and the focus. Call on others to fill in and make a statement. Don't hog the show, but don't relinquish leadership either. Every good band has a leader.

Take accountability for smooth functioning, and at the same time be prepared with something that is easily integrated into the rest of the conversation, yet boldly stands apart.

One-to-a-Small-Group

Tradition states that in groups of five to thirty you will take the floor and even keep it for the entire time you are together. This is a mistake. Make opportunities early on to get interaction. Ask genuine questions—not silly things like, "How many people here are from St. Louis?" Instead, ask relevant questions like, "How many here have heard of our initiative? Who has some doubts about its capacity to make a difference?" Raise your own hand. Join their crowd. Then explain where you are coming from in candid terms.

Always take questions as they arise. Setting aside time for questions and answers (Q&A) is a mistake in any size group. It robs everyone of context, forcing all interaction to happen in isolation; sets you up to end on a less-than-energetic note (since when is Q&A inspiring?); and requires people to listen for more than fifteen minutes at a time, the optimal time span to hold adult attention.

Tell plenty of stories when you have the floor. These are the most memorable and engaging ways to get your points across. Stay away from bullets and PowerPoint. There are those who will say it is the norm, and therefore expected and required. But why should you pander to norms that reflect ineffective tradition or succumb to unsuccessful technique?

One-to-a-Large-Group

You have just graduated to a size where you can guarantee that a third of the audience of thirty to three hundred won't like you or your message for some reason beyond your control: their cat died yesterday, they hate your clothes, you look like their fifth-grade math teacher, or their lunch is disagreeing with them. Another third is probably partially sold on your point of view or won't have trouble with what you are going to say. And the last third is genuinely trying to figure out if you have something of value. You are speaking to this last third.

Provide clear information through stories, giving them the kind of information that you know they are looking for (because you did your homework by reading their Web site, talking to their boss, and interviewing several of them in advance of your presentation). Make it easy for them to decide.

You are not there to convince them but to make it easy for them to evaluate your offer. If you have a genuinely good idea (you do, or you wouldn't be taking the time to read this book), all you have to do is lay out your aspirations and honestly provide the data you have when they ask for it.

Find creative ways to encourage interaction. With a group this size, you will need to ask questions that are relevant and can demand a response before a significant crowd—questions like, "Is it true that geographical distribution is your most difficult challenge?" This safe yes-or-no question is immediately followed up by an open-ended query: "And what are the next two priorities you must address to succeed?"

I always request a wireless *lav* (a lavaliere—a small, lapel microphone) or headset so that I am free to walk about, being responsive to and engaged with the audience. I dispense with a podium, stand, or anything else that physically comes between my listeners and me. I use all aspects of my *instrument* (a theatrical term indicating the capacity of your entire body to express) to connect and communicate. With a larger audience, this full engagement increases the impact and effectiveness of your communication.

One-to-a-Very-Large-Group

When a group climbs over three hundred people, it behaves like a small city. There is always someone somewhere in the audience doing everything that people do in public: eating, talking, pointing, and carrying on. On the perimeter, a steady flow of people in and out of the room.

There will be large I-Mag (image magnification) screens broadcasting your image to the people in the middle and back rows who are watching you as if you are on TV rather than live. Lights are often blinding, making it difficult for you to see much of what is going on, and you will be relying on at least one microphone. It is an intimidating form because of the lack of information you receive from the majority of your audience.

I did not fully understand how to work a crowd this size until eleven hours after my first presentation to eighteen hundred people. I was in Minneapolis as a keynote speaker for the American Society of Association Executives. I spoke first thing in the morning, around 9:00 A.M. At 8:00 P.M. I had the opportunity to watch Jay Leno entertain the same crowd. Here was a consummate professional speaking to the same people I had addressed. I was intensely interested. I stood on the sidelines where I could observe him work and see the audience at the same time.

I watched Leno work the front few rows, the first three hundred people, and let the cameras take care of conveying this interaction to everyone else. He had few encounters with the whole room. For example, when everybody laughed, he paused, waited, and then spoke to everyone, saying something like, "You like that, don't you?" Then he went back to the front rows for his give-and-take.

Here is what I learned from Leno:

- Go to the people you can see and connect with easily—in his case, the first few rows. Make eye contact and banter with them.
- Drive the connection with those who are within normal human range. With them you can rely on your instincts.
- Rely on the camera crew to impart this to everyone else.
- Remain open and responsive when the larger group expresses itself, like the laughter I mentioned.

I have since used these principles with audiences that contain many thousands, and they work well. Never stop listening. Never, *never* give up interaction: it is the stuff of communication. There must be a back-and-forth dialogue. Always be ready to engage. There is nothing like hearing a collective response that lets you know you have reached thousands of people. This alone creates gravity, bringing people to your cause.

Success Rules

- Communicating so people get it and spread it is about creating chain reactions of conversations, where each conversation leads to one or more interactions.
- If you want your idea to spread, you need to become expert at:
  - Leading conversations that engage.
  - Generating cascades of activity.
  - Conducting strategic engagement.
- Elevator speeches only take you down. Leave one-way communication, slogans, and elevator speeches in favor of engaging interactions.

- Inappropriate emphasis on project planning can kill a good idea. Don't fall into this resource sinkhole early on. Instead, get out and talk to people.
- Learn how to lead engaging interactions from the start.
- Jump-start bold conversations.
- Create cascades of conversations.
- Make support materials easily available. Help all eager evangelists to be successful.
- Conduct strategic engagement. Be the conductor in your orchestra.
- Use different techniques for audiences of different sizes.

Energizing Your Most Valuable Players

A select group of people is going to bring your initiative to life. I call these people your *Most Valuable Players* (MVPs). They are not always your friends. They do not always have clout, political power, or resources. But they are powerful in the truest sense of the word and deserve your respect. Your MVPs will midwife the future you are working hard to realize.

In sports an MVP is often isolated from the team, recognized for prowess and performance that goes beyond team playing and exceptional individual achievement. But in a change initiative, your MVPs include every person of influence and anyone who plays for your cause.

Make no mistake: change depends on people. The action people take is the performance that makes things happen. Your MVPs are human beings; blood and guts; hearts, minds, and hands. If you treat them respectfully and appropriately, you will increase the already powerful impact they wield: their ability to wring results from an uncertain future.

Some of your MVPs will emerge completely unsolicited. You may never even meet them. Instead you will hear about them far outside your own sphere of action. When change travels far and wide and outpaces you and your team, this is often the case. However, this does not obviate the need for VIP attention to a special crew. In this chapter you will learn how to identify and tend to your MVPs. I will also highlight three elite forces that deserve the red carpet treatment: your Change Leadership Team, Champions, and Ambassadors.

Jim Wolfensohn on Talking to Everyone

Jim Wolfensohn began his work as president of the World Bank with an ambitious change agenda. When he arrived, he found an organization that was considered by many heads of state to be a necessary but bothersome bureaucracy that was almost irrelevant. He wanted to change that image and establish the World Bank as the preeminent source of knowledge and experience, the first choice a country would turn to when it needed help with its development.

He knew the expertise, know-how, and experience of World Bank staff were exemplary. He also recognized that knowledge was not proprietary to the World Bank. It resided everywhere, including among the poor, the World Bank's beneficiaries. He made it a point to listen to people inside and outside the organization: up, down, and outside the hierarchy. His willingness to include people outside the formal channels sometimes created consternation. Nonetheless, he was highly effective.

I visited about 120 countries where I did not just go to the palaces. I spent the first couple of days in the field before I would ever see the president. That was my usual request: "Get me out in the field first, and then I'll go see the president."

I was not going to say, "Mr. President, I have just come from Washington." Instead I wanted to say, "I have just come from Washington, and I've been out to see the schools in your countryside. This is what is happening there. What do you think of that?"

What did you get from your meetings with local people?

Meeting ordinary people was powerful. I would have illiterate parents come up to me and tell me that they were keeping their child, boy or girl, in the school so he could get his qualifications and the tools to improve his life. That cannot help but move you. That is what gave me the passion for this job and this work.

My job was not just an administrative job. It was about people in poverty whose main vision was to give their children an opportunity. That is what gave me the understanding and passion I have for my work. I have had hundreds, if not thousands, of conversations like that. It changes you. You learn what is happening on the ground.

You made a concerted effort to learn directly from people on the ground.

To bring about change, you cannot just speak with leaders. You have to speak with people at all levels. They have to feel you understand them. And you have to understand the different levels of change that they are serving.

When you talk about change, you have to demonstrate that you are thinking about it at a top policy level, not just announcing a new target, but ensuring there are a plan and resources, financial and human, to attain the objectives.

Identifying Your Most Valuable Players

MVPs come in all roles and functions. They make their appearance up, down, and across the hierarchy. Some make the group through the resources they command or their political clout. Others earn it by delivering powerful results.

Internal and External Core Constituencies

Core constituencies are the groups that must be on board in order for your change to succeed. You will, of course, have core constituencies inside the organization—your *internal core constituencies*. You will probably also have *external core constituencies*—those who reside outside the organization and therefore outside the control of your leadership hierarchy.

CORE CONSTITUENCIES IN A PROGRAM DEALING WITH TRAGEDY

I worked on a government change effort in response to a tragedy. The program was large scale, highly visible, and under tremendous scrutiny by the press as well as internal authority. Our internal core constituencies included departments and divisions in operations, legal, external relations, and research, as well as the senior leadership. Our external core constituencies included the families of the staff who were affected, the general public, the U.S. Congress, and the president of the United States. We needed buy-in from all of these internal and external groups for success.

Once you have identified the groups you must reach, it is time to pinpoint the individuals you will contact to establish relationships. These are your MVPs. You must get to the individual level, building relationships with people.

Categories for Identifying MVPs

A list of categories for you to consider for each constituency follows. Spend time going through the categories, and for each, ask yourself, "Who in this group is instrumental to my success? Who in this group can effectively block or slow down my progress? Who in this group has something to gain or lose when my change gains currency?" The answers to those questions reveal your MVPs.

Keep a written list. I carry one around with me for each initiative I am supporting:

- *Political leaders.* These include members of your organization's senior leadership team and anyone else who holds the power to stop the trains on a whim. Take special note of executive advisors and informal gurus who have your leaders' attention.

- *Policymakers.* Those who create policies that will be important to your results are critical to include. Their participation may be slight, but their impact is huge.

- *Resource providers.* Look closely at those with budget authority, the power to direct and allocate people, and members of the program office who command time assignments.

- *Influencers.* Influencers are the heads of informal groups, old-timers with political savvy, leaders of social networks, people who hold political favors, and coordinators of any group you depend on.

- *Thought leaders.* These are people who are looked to for their expertise in a particular field germane to your program. They are commonly speakers, presenters, and authors, recognized for their deep knowledge, extensive experience, or both. Sometimes they are not skilled in a particular area, but others look to them for guidance nonetheless. Thought followers define thought leaders.

- *Technical experts.* Not always recognized or followed, these are the people who genuinely have the know-how: they are specialists in the industry, domain, or technical area.

- *Researchers and academicians.* Those who conduct and gather quantitative and qualitative findings and those who document relevant knowledge can bring exceptional contributions to the quality of your work. Excluding them can result in ignorance that sabotages your success.

- *Practical visionaries.* These are the people who make innovation happen. Their heads are in the clouds and their feet are on the ground. They see far, and they know how to implement and deliver results regularly.

- *Frontline executers.* In the energy business, these are the folks at the coal face. They are in the trenches and carry out the day-to-day work. Their expertise comes directly from experience. They are firsthand sources, and they and their colleagues form the workforce.

- *Partners.* Partners work collaboratively to make business happen. They are usually in a reciprocal relationship with you, codesigning and often coexecuting activity. If your work changes, theirs must as well. Their work program may not be directly affected, but without their support, your change will encounter additional, and sometimes substantial, obstacles.

- *Alliances.* These are strategic partnerships. Different from *partners* as I have defined them above, these are other units or agencies that have common goals with your group and have agreed to share resources. They often provide additional reach and leverage, multiplying your results, as you do the same for them.

- *Suppliers.* Often overlooked because their relationship is logistical or tactical, suppliers are MVPs for these very reasons. They are part of the nitty-gritty of execution and often must change or shift business processes to keep up with change.

- *Competitors.* Often overlooked except by those who recognize the interdependence of the marketplace, competitors can bring a lot to the table. In many instances, they recognize the value of collaboration as long as you do not share proprietary information or threaten market share.

- *Detractors.* There is a Native American saying, "Bring coyote [the trickster] in the front door, or he will come in the back door and bite you in the @#$!" Here are four benefits detractors will bring to you:

1. They will educate you on your weaknesses. Then you can fortify and bolster your position by addressing the areas they identify.

2. Some will convert and become staunch supporters.

3. Simply by associating with them, you will gain respect and build political clout. Others will appreciate your efforts, and you will become a magnet by virtue of your desire to meet with critics. Some detractors will respect you for this as well. Though they may not support your primary effort, they may become partners in other helpful ways.

4. You build bridges to the disenfranchised. This can be helpful in the most interesting and unexpected of circumstances.

All of these groups together form the web of support that will yield and sustain your transformation. As you identify individuals in each of these categories, keep in mind that your list is dynamic. People will drop off the list and others will join. Day in and day out, there is turnover. Maintain your list, and make it your priority to bring newcomers into the fold.

FOURTEEN CATEGORIES OF MVPS

1. Political leaders
2. Policymakers
3. Resource providers (time, people, money)
4. Influencers
5. Thought leaders
6. Technical experts
7. Researchers and academicians
8. Practical visionaries
9. Frontline executers
10. Partners
11. Alliances
12. Suppliers
13. Competitors
14. Detractors

Activating, Equipping, and Energizing Your MVPs

Activating MVPs

Many MVPs can be turned on like a light bulb. By that, I mean they are dormant until you come along with an invitation to be part of something special. If you make it possible for them to contribute in ways that are meaningful to them, you may observe someone who appears dull and lifeless suddenly perk up and become engaged. This is because many employees are trapped in uninteresting, lackluster jobs that have worn them down. Engaging leadership wakes them up simply by inviting them to give more and get more for themselves in the process.

Other MVPs are already high performers and latch on to great new ideas because that is their way. They pick up whatever innovations make sense and raise the bar on performance—their own and that of their organizations.

To reach the high performers, you need to hang out where they congregate, publish in news media they pay attention to, and send the word out through their social networks. If you know in advance who they are, extend a direct invitation—face-to-face preferably. Voice-to-voice is the next best choice. Then follows all electronic correspondence.

Once you have made contact it is imperative that you engage them (also follow my recommendations in "Creating a Shared Stake in Success" in Chapter One):

How to Activate MVPs

1. *Grab their attention by issuing a challenge.* High performers respond to high goals and extraordinary opportunity. Articulate the big wins your program represents, and invite them to make the biggest contribution by leading the pack.

2. *Make becoming an MVP a professional development opportunity.* Many employees are looking to get ahead, and that means acquiring leadership skills. Participation in your program as an MVP is an ideal way for them to demonstrate their competency, command, and results and thereby stand out from the crowd.

3. *Generate magnetism that will pull people to you.* When you publicize your efforts through presentations, articles, videos, and conversations, talk about your MVPs as an elite force taking advantage of a unique opportunity to excel. Make it clear to others that those who join you are among the best. You will create a magnet that draws interested parties to you.

4. *Tell possible members the leadership potential you see in them.* We all respond to others who see who we are or can be. Make it a point to tell people exactly why you want them on your team. Identify and explicitly communicate their skill and talent and how your program is an opportunity to take it further.

Equipping MVPs

Once people express an interest in helping out, you must provide them with everything they need to succeed. Just as specific tools are needed to do a particular job well, your MVPs need skills, information, and relationships to make their work effective.

THREE CRITICAL PROVISIONS FOR MVPS

- Skills
- Information
- Relationships

Skills: MVPs will be helping you in a variety of ways, from liaising with constituencies to providing logistical support, from engaging influential colleagues to addressing logjams and obstacles. Each MVP will have unique needs as to the skills that will make her efforts most successful. Keep an eye out to provide training or relevant learning materials.

Every MVP is a communicator on your behalf. Teach them how to have engaging conversations (see Chapter Two.)

Information: Make every relevant PowerPoint deck, spreadsheet, and document readily and easily available to your MVPs. Make sure your Web site is easy to access, navigate, and download.

Information flows in at least two directions, so provide regular briefs on your progress. Create a simple indicator, like the daily points for the Dow Jones—one number that describes the total market. Also provide greater granularity to make it easy for them to assess progress and pitch in to help where needed.

Just as important, make it simple for your MVPs to reach you. Provide them an easy-to-remember e-mail address, a phone number where they can get a guaranteed response within ninety minutes, a Web form that is easy to use, and regular face-to-face encounters that include lunches and hallway conversations as well as meetings.

Relationships: Relationships are the most important asset for making change happen and getting ahead. Marry the two so that by participating in your program, people have ample opportunities to build the relationships that lead to their own success.

When you have an audience with the president, invite MVPs. When you bring in a thought leader, a technical expert, or a political leader, bring MVPs along. Develop your social web. Become a social architect, brokering relationships for everyone's benefit.

Energizing MVPs

Emotional moods open and close possibilities. The creativity of those who are down and discouraged dwindles, options seem spare to them, and their energy drops. When they are energized and upbeat, innovation sparkles, opportunities are around every door, and vitality increases.

Make it a point to engage your MVPs in activities that lift their mood, rouse their participation, and open up new horizons to them. To do this, you need to understand the basics of what makes an interaction or event energizing for participants.

FIVE ENERGIZERS FOR MVPS

1. Establish impact.
2. Link personal passion to contribution.
3. Improve your MVPs' situation.
4. Advance the growing edge of your MVPs' vocations.
5. Show your appreciation.

Establish Impact: Nobody likes to go to a meeting when it's clear the outcome will not have impact. The inverse is also true. When it's possible to change the way things done, whether through influence, policy, or access to power, everyone gets pumped.

Do what you can to put the pieces in place required to have real impact. Then tell folks what you have done. For example, if you meet an MVP in the hallway and begin having a conversation about his contribution, you might say, "This work you are doing could radically shift our relationship to the front office, propelling the whole program forward."

When you are putting an event or meeting together, bring in a spokesperson to communicate the impact of the output. For example, bring in the CEO to say, "This work is extremely important to our future. With your recommendations, the senior team will craft policy at our next meeting. We are depending on your best efforts."

Link Personal Passion to Contribution: Find out what turns your MVPs on, and figure out how to make their participation in the change program a way to pursue that.

When I began working on KM with Steve Denning, he found out I was into storytelling and the study of rituals of transformation (coming of age, weddings, and so on). Much to my surprise, we began having conversations about how to use story and ritual in our work. Previously I had delegated my interest to extracurricular activity. My engagement in his program skyrocketed as I started to use storytelling and the principles of ritual in it, and I bought in 100 percent to the program.

Improve Your MVP's Situation: Can you wire your success to your MVP's next promotion? How about making one of your milestones to achieve his unit's target goals? Can you take work off his desk as a result of his participation? What about creating efficiencies that reduce his budget costs or increased performance that results in increasing his revenues?

Make your successes enhance, upgrade, or advance his circumstance. Be explicit. Put their goals on your timeline.

Advance the Growing Edge of Your MVPs' Vocations: Every professional I have worked with takes great pride in his or her field. Create events that push the envelope in each MVP's chosen profession. Bring in outside experts and thought leaders as well as internal gurus. Shape the topics of your events to address the most exciting developments in his domain. Publicize big names and important topics, and request your MVP's attendance out of respect.

Show Your Appreciation: Appreciation is one of the most cost-effective (free) and underused resources available in the work world today. I am referring to taking the time to get to know what is most important in the lives of your MVPs and then expressing your personal appreciation for their efforts.

Here are two examples, from two different spheres:

- An MVP leads a major effort to win new business and succeeds. You bump into her in the hallway and say, "That was a fantastic job you did with our new account. Thanks for putting your best effort into it."
- An MVP has just finished a multiple-day bicycle ride to raise money for cancer. Just before your next meeting, you walk up and say, "I hear you just finished a four-day bike ride for cancer. That's amazing. I really appreciate what you did."

These simple acts, two sentences each, arouse pride and the gratification that comes from being seen by another in a favorable light. The power cannot be understated. In addition, it builds your relationship through acknowledging your MVPs' efforts, and your connecting heart and mind spells success for your continued collaboration.

Extraordinary Envoys

Cultivating three specific groups can provide major returns to you: Change Leadership Team, Champions, and Ambassadors. These are your most powerful agents—the people who drive change as no others can. Each of these three groups is a special action force that can be brought to bear on change. Depending on the size and scope of your program, you may wish to employ more of one than another. (Table 3.1 sets out the characteristics of each of these groups.)

Change Leadership Team members are leaders from each of your major constituencies. I have worked with teams that vary in size from four to fifty, and they have been equally effective and would not hesitate to recommend a larger group if the size of your program and number of core constituents demands it. These team members work together to provide strategic input to the program, and they execute and coordinate change activity across all core constituencies.

Champions are independent actors who represent the change program on the ground within their constituencies. Generally they can be counted on to move initiatives from the central coordination out to the local levels. One thing that distinguishes them from the Change Leadership Team is that they are solo operators. No less instrumental, they provide input and insights.

Ambassadors are representatives of your program and often carry the authority to negotiate and transact business on your behalf. They may or may not be members of the groups they engage.

Change Leadership Team

The members of the Change Leadership Team, drawn from your MVPs, are leaders of your most important constituencies. This group is tasked with building a shared vision and coordinating the activities of your change program across the organization. Building a shared view is the key to creating coherence throughout the system.

This team's mandate is to steer the change as it unfolds. They take the initiative through to its successful conclusion, across the territory of the organization and under varying conditions. This team is responsible for navigating the road, so to speak. They will deal with unanticipated detours, potholes, and shortcuts. They will make the day-to-day decisions responsible for arriving at your destination safe and sound.

Table 3.1   Characteristics of Change Leadership Teams, Champions, and Ambassadors

	Change Leadership Team	Champions	Ambassadors
Who best serves in this role	A member of the group the person represents; someone who is held in high esteem.	A member of the group the person represents; recognized for achieving successful results.	Someone who commands the respect of the group he or she engages. Anyone who is adept at building the needed relationship.
Personality type	Excels in leadership and as a team player.	Forceful, independent, inspiring.	Diplomat with a strong business sense.
Purpose	Provide information on change to their constituents. Rally support for change. Integrate their constituents' activities with the larger effort. Provide local insight to global effort. Enable more effective execution. Work with each other to address issues and generate solutions.	Inspire their constituents. Take initiative to achieve success in local efforts. Represent the change program locally with enthusiasm.	Strengthen a single relationship between the change office and a critical stakeholder group. Negotiate agreements on behalf of the change office. Authorize business arrangements, transactions, and alliances.
Focus	Improve performance at both the local and systemwide levels simultaneously.	Improve performance locally.	Serve a relationship between the change office and a constituency.

Through collaboration, they will bust silos, uniting people from disparate functions and departments to create unique synergies. Because they represent all parts of the organization, they have a unique capacity to connect to customers, members, partners, and other stakeholders. Figure 3.1 provides a graphic illustration of the Change Leadership Team.

FIGURE 3.1 Change Leadership Team

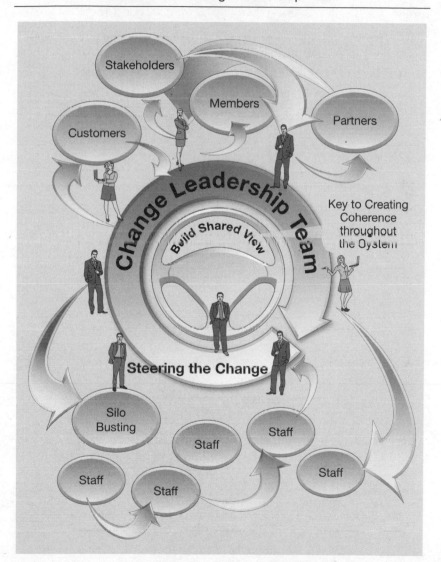

Putting the Team Together: Begin by determining which groups are critical to your success. Then identify members who demonstrate leadership competency and work well in a team environment. Remember that the quality of leadership is improved by bringing together leaders from the most important constituencies.

You may wish to contact the candidates' supervisors in advance. Explain that in exchange, these specially selected individuals will import proficiency in the new changes and develop their leadership capacity.

Make the invitation a special form of recognition. In fact, those who are selected will be on the leading edge of your change program. They will develop a deep understanding of the changes required while simultaneously building their leadership skills. This work positions them well for increased recognition based on the results they initiate and achieve.

Convening the Team: After candidates are selected, bring them together. In the first session, provide team-building activities that are directly related to the work they will be doing together. Most important is to make the Change Leadership Team a learning and professional development opportunity for all members. This means you will be walking the talk of your change program and building leadership skills.

Make sure you put in place processes to:

- Develop the team members' professional skills in accord with the needs of the change program.
- Provide professional recognition for the members.
- Define ground rules and guidelines for team effectiveness.
- Deal with disagreements within the team.
- Remove people from the team should the need arise.
- Report in succinctly to keep members abreast of developments throughout the organization and across their constituencies.

A primary function of this group is to periodically assess the status of the program. This is done not through project management but through cogent check-ins from each member, followed by discussion of critical issues, challenges and solutions.

Optimizing the Change Leadership Team: The purpose of the Change Leadership Team is to bring together leaders from various constituencies to collaboratively lead the initiative. Meet regularly for these reasons:

- Provide support to team members
- Share best practices
- Review progress, individual check-ins, and overall activity
- Identify challenges
- Create solutions

This team is not a democracy. Authority comes from the change office. Therefore, you lead the meetings, choose the topics open for discussion, and run the team.

Ground rules for team effectiveness should be discussed, and most include these:

- Confidentiality when requested, so members can speak candidly about difficult or politically charged issues
- Mutual support, that is, working together to achieve group success
- Consistent participation in a mutually agreed-on schedule
- A method for handling disagreements within the team

Basic expectations should be established in advance for decision making in a variety of situations:

- When you as the Change Leader make the decision
- When you make a decision but with discussion by the team and its advice
- When there should be group discussion and the majority rules
- When there should be group discussion and consensus is required—that is, most team members agree and others can live with the decision.
- When unanimous consent is required

Running the Team: Concise reporting will keep members abreast of developments throughout the organization and across constituencies.

It is often the case that basic questions around purpose and effectiveness are brought up over and again during the course of the change program. You don't want to continually revisit decisions unless changes in circumstances require them. However, I caution you about cutting these conversations short. They form an integral part of the social construction required to achieve excellent results.

Allow members the opportunity to revisit basic assumptions in light of new developments and emerging insights. This is a far-reaching conversation when conducted among your change leaders. The opportunity to meet and challenge core views can have a tremendous positive impact, including strategic reevaluation and a robust common understanding among your MVPs. Strategic reevaluation occurs when well-informed people with relevant experience think together about the consequences of their work. If the emotional tone is constructive, tremendous value can emerge.

EXAMPLES OF DISCUSSION OUTCOMES

- You realize that a core constituency has been marginalized by your approach. You now have the opportunity to modify your activity and rectify the situation.
- Unintended consequences are identified. You now have the opportunity to harvest potential wins previously unseen or avoid an unanticipated train wreck.
- New possibilities for dramatic increases in performance or accelerated early successes are spotted.

Repeated discussions of basic approaches and concepts can fortify the understanding of the entire team. This happens by deepening individual understanding with the input of trusted peers.

A more robust common understanding results as members of the team integrate their frontline experience. This happens when they share their insights, perceptions, appreciations, and judgments with the other members of the team. As a result of this stronger common understanding, individual behavior takes on a greater coherency within the group, which leads to increased effectiveness and resilience, especially when challenging situations arise.

All in all, the Change Leadership Team is one of the most effective groups of MVPs. The team members connect core constituencies, facilitate a shared understanding across the effort, bust silos as needed, and steer transformation in a complex environment.

Champions

Some individuals excel at promoting, advocating, and supporting change within their home group, that is, the constituency in which they reside. These are powerful allies you can draw on to help floundering projects, marshal resources for high-value opportunities, and inspire local efforts. Champions come in all shapes. Many think of champions as type A personalities, driven and consumed by the pursuit of success. But this is not always the case. They can be quiet advocates who do the behind-the-scenes work to ensure success or data-driven analysts who advocate for and advise on evidence-based practices for your cause.

It is a great day when you discover Champions among constituencies who need the extra effort. Get to know the person behind the force. Find out what motivates her. Use your engagement skills to generate possibilities for win-wins. "Eight Conversations That Create the Future" in Chapter One provide excellent questions to kick off a conversation with your Champions.

A word of caution: some Champions want to be handled lightly, some want tight integration, and others can be anywhere within the continuum. Figure 3.2 illustrates the continuum of participation.

Ambassadors

Ambassadors are empowered to represent you in their dealings with other groups. They serve a valuable function, extending your reach

FIGURE 3.2 Continuum of Champions' Participation

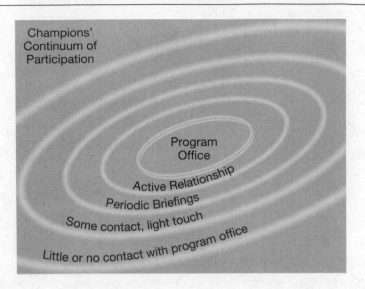

Champions'
Continuum of
Participation

Program
Office

Active Relationship

Periodic Briefings

Some contact, light touch

Little or no contact with program office

and increasing your ability to negotiate favorable conditions and even business. In a change program, Ambassadors typically take on this role because it provides them with special standing. Often they are not compensated or otherwise formally acknowledged in their job description. Essentially this is a volunteer activity that increases their status in your program and with the group they are liaising with on your behalf.

You should at all times be on the lookout for Ambassadors to represent your cause. To identify them, first ask yourself which other groups you need to be able to conduct business with or influence. Perhaps there is an internal unit like HR or your strategy council that you need to negotiate with. Or maybe you want to open up deliberations with a critical external partner. If so, take note of who emerges as a trustworthy representative, and consider bestowing Ambassador status on that person.

To do this effectively, you must be explicit about the power you are extending and your intentions. Often Ambassadors receive elite status in exchange for their role. Consider what you have to offer to make it worth their while. You may wish to consider creating a special

Ambassadors' Club to provide best practices and recognition among the representatives.

USING AMBASSADORS TO ACHIEVE A GOAL

I worked once with an informal group in a public agency that felt they were being treated unfairly. They wanted better treatment and had a variety of special causes to champion. They chose not to litigate but instead self-organized, discussed their cause collectively, strategized as to the best way to put pressure on the agency, and took unified, coordinated action.

Several members of the group worked in influential positions around the agency. The larger group authorized each of these people to negotiate on its behalf. Trust was high, and the goals were articulated clearly. These people were Ambassadors of the movement. Their unique positions made them particularly effective in this role. Because they had been explicitly given authority to negotiate, they were free to make binding arrangements. They were highly effective as independent agents and generated a broad range of coordinated effort.

Difficult Players: Apathetic, Cynical, and Antagonistic

I have written about detractors and competitors, but I turn special attention toward those who are in critical roles and don't care about your program, see it through skeptical eyes, or display animosity toward it. These people can nevertheless be MVPs in their own right. How you handle these challenges requires special consideration. There is great opportunity here. If it is squandered, it can backfire and set you back considerably. Yet with a clear focus and strong position, you can often turn these challenges to your advantage.

If you have a good, strong idea or change program, you will have detractors—those who think you are on the wrong track and take up forces against you. They can be dealt with effectively as I have laid out earlier in this chapter. However, if people begin to treat you poorly, you have a different kind of problem. This includes those who say or demonstrate through their behavior:

- I don't care about you, your program, or what you do.
- Nothing works in this awful place. Every initiative including yours is doomed to fail.
- I don't like you or what you stand for, and I will take you down when I get the chance.

Remember what you are doing. This is about effecting change; it is not about personal warfare. If you degenerate into personal warfare, you and your program will suffer as a consequence.

If you find yourself drawn in emotionally, you need to take care of yourself so you can help those around you. If you are overtaken with animosity in response, you have become ensnared in an emotional diversion and are no longer leading change.

I will give you a way out that is based on action, but you need to get centered first. Here are some suggestions to adjust your attitude:

- *Explore why this person is causing an intense reaction.* She may be triggering a response that really has nothing to do with what she is saying but some element of your own experience. If so, find someone to talk it through with: a close friend, your spouse, or a counselor. There is probably productive material emerging that will make you stronger and more able. A confidant can be invaluable in taking this conundrum to a productive conclusion.
- *Exercise.* Work out, go to the gym, or take a walk. In short, do activities that you enjoy and get your body moving. This is a great way to blow off stress and get perspective on the issue. Exercise is one of the fastest, most rewarding ways to shift consciousness into a productive state-of-mind.
- *Kick yourself in the rear.* Sometimes all you need to do to get moving is ask yourself to play a bigger game and move on. You

may simply have been diverted, and an inner pep talk may help you refocus and get back to work.

Risk/ROI Matrix for Difficult People

To decide how important it is to engage the person or people who are treating you with indifference, cynicism, or animosity, use the RISK/ROI matrix.

Risk represents the possibility that something unwanted will occur as a result of this person's behavior or influence. Low risk means that it is unlikely he will inflict damage to your initiative. High risk means he probably will wreak significant havoc through his views or actions.

ROI represents the potential value this person can generate. Low ROI means that if you win his support, the resulting positive impact is minimal. High ROI means that you could win big if you garner his buy-in.

Using these two factors, we can create a matrix that is useful, as in Figure 3.3. Let's look at each of the quadrants in the matrix:

FIGURE 0.0 Risk/ROI Matrix for Difficult People

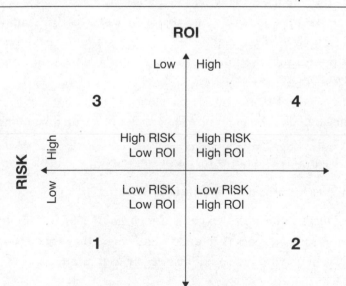

Low risk, Low ROI	There is little chance these stakeholders pose a threat, and if you win them and their support, the resulting benefit is small. Leave them alone until they move into another quadrant.
Low risk, High ROI	These people are not likely to inflict damage, and yet they offer significant rewards. Engage them, and attempt to win them over. Failing that, try to build a relationship with them.
High risk, Low ROI	These people are prone to aggressively come after your program, and there is little to be gained from winning their support. If the damage they inflict is significant, work to diffuse their impact. Otherwise devote your efforts to your priorities.
High risk, High ROI	Here you have people who are likely to inflict damage on your program but can provide significant returns if they are converted. Even if you only partially win them over (perhaps they support one part of your program, but not another), they can bring real benefits. They are a priority.

Special Advice for Working with Apathetics and Cynics

Generally these people have a chip on their shoulder that has to do with their ability to influence or wield their expertise effectively. I have had great success by acknowledging their experience and know-how and inviting them to use it to bolster the change work.

Often skeptics and those who appear to be slackers are simply operating in a toxic environment themselves. By extending the opportunity to contribute and have impact, you can win them over and even fully energize them in a positive way.

In 75 percent of the cases I have encountered, apathetic, cynical, and antagonistic people can be overcome with personal handling. This is an extraordinary percentage. This means the issue is how they are perceived and treated rather than insurmountable opposition.

Techniques for Engaging Difficult People

1. *Tell them you want to understand their point of view.* Simply communicating your desire to understand where they are coming from will gain you ground and diffuse negative emotions.

2. *Make a strong attempt to hear them out.* Their story is always valid from their point of view. Put effort into understanding how they came to their position. Suspend your assumptions, and work to put yourself in their shoes.

3. *Ask them how you can work together, and offer suggestions.* Initiate a collaborative approach, and offer your best thinking as a place to start. Be quick to follow their lead.

4. *Be honest about where there is disagreement.* Once you have engaged them, do not sacrifice your goals and intentions. Instead, in the spirit of honesty, make clear where you part paths.

Each of these strategies is aimed toward diffusing emotional antagonism. Success includes turning these people into constructive detractors; those who do not support your efforts, but will engage with you in a supportive manner.

Suppose you have done all of this, and they still write you off or are out to get you? What then?

Options for Working with Toxic and Unredeemable People

1. *Go around them.* Seek support from their peers. Build an alliance across their social network, and go through others to influence or neutralize their behavior.

2. *Go over them.* Address the issues with their superiors. Once you win support, explore how to minimize the risk associated with them.

3. *Go under them.* Establish working relationships with their subordinates. This is risky for the subordinates, so you must offer them protection—perhaps anonymity or otherwise shield them from harm.

4. *Go through them.* At every engagement, show up prepared to do judo: take their assaults and turn the force toward your objectives.

5. *Wall them off.* Isolate them from their points of influence. Do this by identifying their partners—those they work with to generate negative impact for your program—and engage each of them.

USING JUDO ON AN OPPONENT

I once met with a department director who was dead set against the change work my client was leading. He claimed the effort was counter to the mission of the organization. After a short conversation, it became apparent that he saw no role for himself in the future if our effort was successful. I asked him to participate in some of our strategy sessions and raise the mission issue with an eye to how he could personally ensure that we were consistent with the organization's mission.

By inviting him in, I hoped to draw on his energy and focus it on our goal. He refused to participate. But several of his subordinates who were present for our encounter attended, offered helpful suggestions, and became advocates. His attacks on us soon faded away altogether. I call this "judo" because I did not push against his force but instead used it toward constructive ends.

In all cases, be aware that your actions are visible to many people, and the way you run your program makes one of the most powerful statements in support of your eventual success. If you do your best to engage the difficult, winning some over, and then working strategically, without hostile intent, to take corrective action with those who do not engage, you will garner respect and support from many observers.

The goal is always on success, not winning everyone over. Detractors are welcome to engage productively. The merits of the program and your approach are your ultimate tools. Keep your eyes on this rather than on personalities who stand in your way.

Success Rules

- Your Most Valuable Players are the people who will breathe life into your initiative.

- Activating, equipping, and energizing your MVPs are high-impact actions you can take to increase their effectiveness and spread your program.
- Create three groups that will have a particularly high impact: the Change Leadership Team, Ambassadors, and Champions.
- When key people are apathetic, cynical, or antagonistic, turn to productive ways of engaging them.

Understanding the Territory of Change

Maps help travelers avoid difficult areas or prepare for them. They make it possible to weigh the advantages of the long route versus the short one. And when unplanned interruptions crop up, they can get you where you need to go in short order.

Mapping the territory of change, however, is easier said than done. It requires taking into account varieties of intelligence: individual and collective, logistical and political, cultural and technical. The best way to get a good layout of the land is to use a systematic approach of scouting, gathering intelligence, and exploring the periphery. I also rely a great deal on intuition—my own and that of the people I speak with.

Scouting, Reconnaissance, and the Avant-Garde

Scouting, reconnaissance, and the *avant-garde* are military terms that take on new meaning when they are applied to organizational change.

Scouting means exploring the way ahead, going into the unknown and the uncertain to discover a safe way forward. *Reconnaissance* is the gathering of information useful to achieve the advantage for engagement. And the *avant-garde,* in its common English use, refers to those who are innovative and experimental. All three are about preparing for the future by seeking to understand what is coming up ahead.

Scouts deliberately go into the frontier. They take risks so that others can prepare for what is likely to come, including progress along the trail.

Conducting reconnaissance in the military sometimes means going behind enemy lines, a risky proposition, to say the least. But it justifies the effort and potential high cost with a wealth of information that generates significant advantage.

The avant-garde is known for its strange forays into the fringe, where glimpses of the future can be caught mingled with false starts and random bits of creative expression. Experiments in art provide new and different perspectives that foreshadow social trends, innovations, and new ways of being.

All of these entail purposefully venturing into the unknown to gather useful perspectives. Their payoffs can be immense, but they are not for the faint of heart. By talking to people who offer other perspectives and critiques, you can map the territory of your change as your MVPs perceive it. This information allows you to chart challenges and opportunities and describe what may be needed to navigate relationships, negotiations, and business processes to achieve successful results successfully.

A number of benefits come from understanding the territory of change:

1. *Preparation for successful implementation.* You see all the big issues and themes at play as you prepare. This inside information is what you need to put together a workable approach.
2. *An increased ability to address needs.* By gathering this inside information, you can see the world through others' eyes so that you can answer their concerns and improve their situation in ways they appreciate.
3. *Identification of possible risks.* The best risk management is being informed about where you can run into difficulty, become derailed, stir up trouble, collide with other activities or circumstances, or face significant challenges.

4. *Bringing unspeakable or taboo topics into the open.* The territory includes obvious truths that are being ignored or going unaddressed yet have an impact on your ability to deliver results. By bringing them into the open, you have a much higher likelihood of dealing with them effectively.

5. *Gaining feedback on critical issues, creating receptivity to solutions.* This benefit enables you to get clear about what is and is not important, where there is energy and where there isn't, what will be difficult and what will be easy, what requires resources to address and what solutions already exist.

6. *Identification of high-value wins.* As the territory becomes clearer, opportunities come into sharp focus.

7. *Educational requirements that become clear.* Often information that is needed for effective engagement is missing . An understanding of the environment of change helps identify and address educational deficits.

Recently I helped a large financial firm design a conference for its top salespeople nationwide. These thirty people and their staff of seventy were responsible for billions of dollars in sales.

The purpose of my involvement was to shift the conference from an annual obligation to a knowledge-sharing fest that engaged the sales reps. The goal was for them to want to improve their performance collectively. Most of these salespeople were experts, highly motivated, and always eager to improve their own performance. Caring about the rest of the team and group performance was another thing.

According to the vice president and senior vice president who presided over the event, this event was the most engaging conference they ever had. It kicked off a year of activities to identify and harvest the collective intelligence for all.

A major contribution to the success of the three-day event was the information I gathered in advance by talking to sixteen members of the sales team. These short conversations, none longer than thirty minutes, provided a clear picture of the challenges they were facing, the answers they were looking for, their history, and their ideals of success. Especially important, they provided the opportunity to assess their attitudes toward the annual conference, the company, their peers, managers, and the senior team. Bringing together this information in a single, holistic Reconnaissance Report enabled me to foresee challenges, identify solutions, and address concerns before planning the meeting. (A sample of such a report appears later in this chapter.)

As a neutral party operating in an environment of confidentiality, I was privy to perspectives not otherwise shared. As themes emerged, I identified the obvious truths that were going unaddressed or unacknowledged and could design interactions that raised these issues constructively without putting any one person at risk.

Most organizations skimp on gaining this invaluable information or skip it altogether, to their detriment. Building trust and listening to MVPs systematically is a powerful tool for creating engagement, acceptance, and buy-in.

Storylistening, the complement to storytelling, is key.

Storylistening

Storylistening is paying careful attention to another's storytelling. Reconnaissance using eight storylistening skills and accomplishes two important goals simultaneously: gathering valuable information from the most important stakeholders and building trust among those same people:

Eight Storylistening Skills

1. *Listen with purpose.* You are listening to (1) build trust and (2) gather relevant information, in that order. If you build trust but do not gain all of the needed information, it will be easy to go back as needed and pick up what you didn't get the first time. However, if you gather information but fail to create rapport grounded in mutual respect, you may not be able to count on the information you have retrieved, and likely there won't be any more conversations.

2. *Use effective body language, even on the phone.* When you are on the phone, arrange your body as you do when you are listening in person. I don't know why it works, but it does. I've heard it said, "If you're not happy, smile. You soon will be happy." And I've found it to be true. Paying attention with your entire being, even if a phone line separates you, will improve the quality of your listening.

3. *Follow the stories.* Narrative is a natural structure. Stories inevitably point the way toward what the person cares about most—her observations, insights, and conclusions.

4. *Affirm the validity of the MVP's expertise, experience, and professional assessments.* Every professional has dedicated years and even decades to establishing and developing competencies within a domain of knowledge. Yet in ordinary conversation, many are quick to dismiss it. In conversations throughout the workday, others may minimize your teller's experience and expertise. Affirming the validity of the person's knowledge and experience, even if you don't agree with him, opens the way to a more candid and revealing interaction. You may say something like, "Given your fifteen years in the oil and gas industry, and especially your experience in the Gulf of Mexico, I am appreciative of the opportunity to get your views on this."

5. *Ask questions to guide the interaction.* You are there to listen and learn. Rather than making statements or elaborating on your own observations, ask questions. To learn about customer service, for example, ask, "And how important is customer service in your work? What are the most important aspects of customer service as you see them? What have been the biggest issues with customer service so far? Do you think improved customer service would address that?"

6. *Seek clarification.* Don't take judgments at face value. Inquire to reveal what's behind attitudes, feelings, perceptions, and insights.

7. *Confirm what you hear.* Repeat back what you heard, and ask the teller to either confirm your understanding or amend it.

8. *Express appreciation to the teller for her efforts.* Gratitude goes a long way toward building trust and rapport and can begin by thanking the

person for this time. At the conclusion, say something like, "I really appreciate this conversation. It has helped the effort considerably."

Madelyn Blair on Storylistening for Reconnaissance

Madelyn Blair is expert in the fields of organizational development, knowledge management, instructional design, and research technique and the author of *Riding the Current: True Stories and Tested Techniques for Keeping Your Knowledge Fresh and Your Work Alive.*[1] She designed and created the methodology of information flow analysis, which her organization, Pelerei, has used to create information strategies that are easy to understand and efficiently developed.

She is a former division chief for the World Bank. Her mastery comes from listening to thousands of stories in the line of her work. Madelyn contributes widely to the fields of applied storytelling and social construction.

The key to using stories to gather information, to understand the territory of change, is to know that stories carry more than words and facts. When you listen to people's stories, you are giving them a chance to express in multiple media, multiple dimensions.

Stories carry emotional information, hopes, desires, intentions, and bits and pieces of relevant information subtly connected to successful change work. It is as though by listening, you are weaving together the teller's experience with the intentions of the change process, transforming both. When you step into a new environment, you want to appreciate it at every level in order to work within it effectively. Stories are a powerful tool for getting as close as you can to seeing through the eyes of the people you are talking to.

You need to learn how to drop your own assumptions and take on those of the people you are listening to. It is not always easy, but the reward is profound. A new world emerges that includes both the teller and the listener in new ways. In a recent engagement, a member of the client team was resistant to change at the same time that he needed the change most intensely. To break through, I asked him to tell me a story about his situation—an example that would help me understand it better. He tended to talk at the intellectual level of generalities. As he talked, I asked for examples. I wanted to hear the story of his experience. As he unfolded his story, I understood it better. Then something amazing happened: he became more open to me as I began to understand what he was saying. As a result, I was able to effect tremendous change. When you are in a very tough situation, you need to take the time to go and listen to people's stories with a deep sense of curiosity and openness so you can really become connected to them.

The Reconnaissance Report

A Reconnaissance Report is a one- to two-page document that synthesizes your interviews and all you've learned from them. It highlights the themes, concerns, educational needs, and opportunities that are shared across the group or are critically important. Using these interviews to generate a Reconnaissance Report provides powerful benefits:

Six Benefits of the Reconnaissance Report

1. *It serves to document the territory of change.* It is a record and a snapshot of important themes, perceptions, issues, and challenges during a particular time span.
2. *It jump-starts trust building.* People recognize it as an honest attempt to capture all important issues and concerns. Reading their own words or seeing extrapolations that are close to what they intended to convey validates the authenticity of the communication, which builds trust.
3. *It continues their participation and contribution.* Through the interview, MVPs begin to contribute to the initiative. This documentation of their contributions publicly acknowledges the value they're offering.

4. *It is a targeted conversation starter.* The Reconnaissance Report is a useful document as a conversation starter, serving as a menu of relevant issues that can be addressed.
5. *It is especially helpful for addressing the elephants in the room.* These are the important and obvious topics that everyone is aware of but are not discussed because they are uncomfortable to address.
6. *It captures the attitudes and observations creating a logjam, bottleneck, or stall.* Understanding the causes of a logjam will help you to address it successfully.

The Reconnaissance Report encapsulates the storylistening results by including quotes from the interviews. You can do this by recording the sessions, if you have enough initial trust with your interviewees, or handwriting important statements made by the MVPs. Recording is the better option for three reasons: (1) you don't really know what is important until you have had a chance to listen to everyone, (2) recordings capture comments in the flow and context of the conversation, and (3) they offer perfect recall so you can quote the words exactly as they were said.

Of course, recording sometimes is not possible. So in those instances, just write down what you hear as best you can.

To produce the Reconnaissance Report, listen for five important types of information during the storylistening sessions. These *five gems* are invaluable in understanding the territory of change. When more than one person is conducting the interviews, these five gems serve as a common framework, making it easier to compare and compile results.

Five Gems to Gather Through Storylistening

1. *Red lights.* These are showstoppers as perceived by the people being interviewed—reasons they believe the initiative will fail. The interviewee might say, "Let me tell you why this will never work."
2. *Yellow lights.* These are cautions. They point to challenges and obstacles that require action to be averted. You might hear, "If we

don't include HR in this, there's going to be trouble!" or "We haven't taken the time to do our due diligence. If we don't get that done, we could be shot down."

3. *Themes.* A theme is anything that more than one person talked about. It need not be rational or real, only in circulation. If more than one person interpreted circumstances in a similar way, it was worth identifying and raising.

4. *Educational deficits.* These are information gaps that need to be filled for people to participate effectively.

5. *High-value nuggets.* Often MVPs will identify major wins that the change leader had not noted previously. These are collected and fed back into the program, to everyone's delight.

FILLING AN EDUCATIONAL DEFICIT

When I was working on a technology pilot, it became clear that several of the people responsible for deciding whether to go ahead had no idea how the technology actually worked. This was unacceptable, so we remedied it by a short presentation conducted by their peers who had a clear understanding.

A six-step process will lead to an effective Reconnaissance Report:

Six Steps to Creating the Reconnaissance Report

1. Identify a representative group of MVPs.

2. Request their time for a short interview, guaranteeing them anonymity.

3. Have a neutral party conduct the interviews, focusing on building trust, understanding their point of view, and gathering the five gems.

4. Take notes including quotes.

5. Review and synthesize the results, looking for patterns and including support quotes.

6. Create a document no longer than two pages, one page front and back, that contains four items:

- Statement of purpose

- Description of what was done

- List of names of those who were interviewed. These may include organizational designation or partner affiliation in a larger organization. In a smaller company or insular group where the names are easily recognized, it is not necessary.

- A synthesis of what was learned

This is a sample Reconnaissance Report. The name of the agency has been changed to provide anonymity.

SAMPLE RECONNAISSANCE REPORT

The purpose of these interviews is to clarify the issues and construct the best path forward for the Performance Improvement Program (PIP). Implementation has stalled. After an initial period that included nine months of enthusiastic support, strategy sessions, and action plans, most activity has come to a halt.

This page represents the findings of a series of interviews conducted among employees and partners associated with forward progress of the PIP. An external consultant and performance improvement specialist conducted the interviews April 15–27 this year.

Those interviewed: Deepak Asthana, Sales Management and Delivery; Maxine Billard, Sales Performance; David Dawson, HR and Legal; Sven Dirksen, Sales Partner; Max Donaldson, HQ Strategy; Larry Gold, Performance Metrics; Manuel Gonzalez, Information Technology; Rachel Jankowksi, Senior Advisor to the CEO; Elaine Perogski, Oversight; Raj Purthi, Operations; Paul Resp, Sales Partner; Julia Rodrigez, Sales Partner; Maria Sanchez, Distribution; Jessica Thornbill, Sales Manager.

- Funding has been withdrawn from key partners, making resource commitments difficult or impossible to carry out.

"All of my funding dried up overnight. I had to redeploy several critical resources or run the risk of losing all hope of a return on their activity. It was a nightmare!"

"The CEO of our partner called me late at night and told me he had no choice but to withdraw funding from this program. He could not justify the investment in his own mind."

"I am barely holding on to my original commitments. They have all been scaled back. The next step is to take out the knife. All this because the money we were promised was withdrawn."

- Enthusiasm for the PIP remains high. People still want to see the goals realized.

"I love what we created."

"If this goes down, I want to find out another way to achieve these objectives. I am married to these wins!"

"The strategy and tactics fit my unit's goals like a glove. We may not go forward with the enterprise-wide version of PIP, but I'll be looking for a way to implement here one way or another."

- Inadequate funding reflects a lack of commitment from key partners.

"I thought the folks in the alliance were completely bought in. I was shocked to see them pull out."

"Apparently some of our most critical partners do not understand the value proposition."

- More than half of those interviewed suspect our senior management dropped the ball:

"This could have been addressed at the highest levels. Why didn't the CEO intervene? I am guessing he is ambivalent, which means he does not understand what this is really about."

"I think the ball got dropped upstairs. I suspect there are political games being played here and we are casualties."

Case Study: Program Supervision Foundation

In 2005, I was contacted by the Program Supervision Foundation (PSF) for help reenrolling disaffected volunteer leaders. (All of the names have been changed for this case study.)

PSF had been experiencing exponential growth over the last several years due to an increasing domestic need for the certification it provided and accelerated international expansion. As membership and revenues increased dramatically, it moved from a volunteer-run organization to full-time paid staff. The turnover was abrupt by necessity as income and service demand spiked. The transition was not smooth, and many of the former volunteer leaders were angered by their sudden lack of power. They resented the staff openly and made a point of criticizing them publicly.

Although the new senior leadership team was upset by this behavior, they recognized that these former leaders had much of the institutional memory, strong social networks, and valuable expertise. As legitimate thought leaders in the profession, they were valuable to the organization but needed to be won over.

The organization itself was in rapid change. It was difficult to keep pace with the growing administrative needs, let alone the needs of the members.

PSF sought a change that would garner the support of the former leaders and engage them in the future strategy of the organization. I was asked to lead a two-day working session to help construct positive relations between the disaffected and the new director of membership services. The new director was on the road constantly, meeting new members and helping fledgling local groups get started. She met with the old guard whenever she could, but they were one-to-one sessions, and the pace of these meetings was too slow.

There was a need to bring everyone together in one place at one time to address their grievances, declare them resolved, and move on, with as many proclaiming full support as possible.

Time was short. Growth was strong. The sooner the previous leaders could be brought on board, the faster their endorsements, collective intelligence, and individual efforts could be brought to bear on the rapidly expanding organization to its members benefit.

Inviting the Volunteer Leaders

A paper invitation went out from the CEO to the thirty-four former leaders inviting them to a special session to assist with the strategic development of PSF. Here is the text of that invitation:

> PSF Global Operations would like to extend you an invitation to participate in an interactive discussion and information-gathering session on the future of the Program Supervision Foundation. This event is scheduled for June 8–10 and will be held in New Orleans, Louisiana. PSF will provide your airfare and lodging.
>
> This two-and-a-half-day meeting will bring together a vital stakeholder group, PSF's past volunteer leaders and members of PSF's Global Operations, to discuss the strategic vision of the organization.
>
> *Background.* PSF's global community, which has experienced incredible growth over the past two years, has created a network of close to three hundred chapters. Moving forward, PSF must ensure that this tremendous resource for the organization is aligned with its strategic vision: "Worldwide organizations will embrace, value, and use program supervision and attribute their success to it."
>
> To pursue this objective, PSF initiated the Strategic Transformation Project on at the start of this year. This is a multiphased project that will deliver a framework for identifying, validating, and supporting PSF community models to meet stakeholder needs and alignment with strategic and market drivers. Phases I and II are being conducted simultaneously: they are researching and evaluating current communities within PSF, including virtual membership groups. From this research, we will develop the framework for our organizational structure to be delivered to the PSF board of directors on November 1.
>
> *Meeting Objectives.* The objective of this meeting is to identify the most valid working structure to ensure the resources and activities of the organization align with and support PSF's strategic direction. Since the inception of PSF's charter agreement and independent incorporation

requirement, we have seen some groups flourish, and others struggle to deliver consistent member value and service. The questions we will explore are: What is the basic function or premise for PSF communities? What model would best support consistent and successful function?

Your experience as a past leader of the organization will be invaluable to the success of this meeting. I hope you will join us.

Expected Outcomes: It is our intent to capture key thoughts and ideas for collectively advancing the profession of program supervision and PSF that will help build the framework to ensure successful achievement of the envisioned goal. At the conclusion of the meeting, individuals will be asked to communicate to their fellow members and capture responses and feedback to the questions posed during this meeting.

We will discuss what works and what doesn't in a professional and objective manner. While it will be important to discuss collectively the historical operational issues, including the transformation from a volunteer to paid-staff operations, we will not allow agenda hijacking to discuss individual issues with PSF policies.

I hope that you will be able to attend this important discussion, as this project will directly affect the future state of PSF.

Rakesh Sharma
CEO, Program Supervision Foundation

Just after the invitation was sent, an e-mail went out to each member with this text:

Greetings,

I want to personally thank you for taking time from your busy schedule to participate in our meeting in New Orleans June 8–10. We are looking forward to working with you in what promises to be a very productive and busy few days.

To ensure that our session is as productive as possible, I am bringing in Seth Kahan to help lead the day. Seth is an experienced strategist who has worked with leaders in world-class organizations such as the Peace Corps, the World Bank, the Fulbright Association, NASA and many others. His expertise in the development of community-based models for organizational growth will be a great asset for our gathering. You can learn more about him through his Web site, www.SethKahan.com.

Seth would like to talk with you briefly about your expectations and hopes for the meeting in New Orleans, and so I have passed along your contact information to him. I would greatly appreciate it if you would take the time for a fifteen-minute phone conversation with him in the next few days. He will be contacting you directly to set that up. I know your ideas and insights will help us to better prepare, and help in the overall success of this meeting. Please be assured that you can share with him in confidence.

I have included the original meeting invitation that outlines the meeting objectives and expected outcomes for your reference. Thank you in advance for your time with Seth.

I look forward to seeing you in New Orleans,

Maria Sanchez
Director, Membership Services

Several important points can be made about the invitation and the letter. Each is an important factor, improving the ability to gather information. This deep understanding of the territory of change will make it possible to design a powerful meeting, addressing concerns and advancing the change agenda.

The Invitation: A formal paper invitation from the CEO, not a form letter or an e-mail, carries weight: this is official business. Furthermore, by paying for airfare and lodging, the CEO is making it clear that he values the members' time. By stating the background, meeting objectives, and expected outcomes upfront, the CEO makes a business case for the session. The healing of old wounds will take place in the business needs of current expansion. This is an important statement, creating a value-based context for going forward.

The second-to-last paragraph references "professional and objective manner" and the disallowance of "agenda hijacking." Agenda hijacking had been a regular practice by the disaffected. This had been accompanied by emotional outbursts, including screaming. Therefore, the CEO felt it necessary to state this in advance.

The second-to-last paragraph is also the first and only reference to discussing "collectively the historical operational issues, including the transformation from a volunteer to paid-staff operations." It was not left to be understood by implication, but instead was made explicit.

The E-Mail: In contrast to the CEO's formal invitation, this message is more casual. Sent through e-mail and beginning with "Greetings," it sets a relaxed tone. These two different styles work well together to convey both the serious business of the matter at hand, and the desire to build bridges:

- I am established as a legitimate professional with relevant experience. This provides structure in an otherwise difficult interaction, lowering the anxiety and building confidence in the outcome.
- The time requested is short, fifteen minutes, so as not to seem onerous.
- Confidentiality is established to encourage honesty.
- Gratitude is expressed to convey respect, which is genuine. Though there have been tense confrontations, the staff do indeed hope to reconcile and bring these wayward leaders back on board.

The Interviews

I followed up immediately and scheduled my conversations. My goal was to complete all conversations within two weeks, giving Maria and me time to integrate what we learned, respond proactively where needed—setting the meeting up for success and, where necessary, reorienting expectations or diffusing tensions.

Prior to my storylistening calls, Maria went through the list of thirty-four with me one by one, explaining each person's history, professional standing, relationship to other leaders in the organization, and position on the current situation.

This time with Maria was, in fact, my first storylistening interview. I listened for the Five Gems carefully as she spoke. She was, of course, one of the MVPs. I learned a great deal about her predilections and biases through this work together.

The rest of the storylistening interviews took place over the next two weeks. About half of them were fifteen to twenty minutes in length. Two were shorter. The rest were around thirty minutes. People did not hold back. I often got an earful. Though people treated me with respect, they were quick to air grievances and anger.

As a result of these interviews, I identified the following themes:

- People are passionate, dedicating their personal time and energy to delivering tangible value to members and the work of leading their communities. They want clear mechanisms for contributing to the evolution of PSF.

- The changing roles of leadership within PSF have been difficult. Yet there has been experimentation with new approaches at the local level, including liaisons with other organizations. Many of these efforts are bearing significant fruit.

- There are many gems—insights and ideas—that have not been shared widely because the current infrastructure doesn't make it easy for volunteer leaders and PSF to collaborate and share knowledge broadly. People want the opportunity to share know-how and experience across the organization.

- In the global marketplace, it is clear that PSF does not own program supervision; rather, PSF is part of a larger constellation. Nevertheless, PSF is positioned well to work synergistically with many of the other associations, corporations, countries, and new partners to achieve its strategic goals and growth.

- People know that global growth represents a unique opportunity for the local communities and volunteer leaders and recognize that everyone will be transformed in the process. There is concern about the continuity of identity, ensuring the capacity to build on existing value for members and a desire to continue traditions of intellectual leadership.

- People feel constraints in the current circumstances. Yet the very issues that are causing uneasiness are precisely those that point the way to successful evolution.

It is important to note no hostility was expressed through these themes; however, legitimate concerns were raised in the context of the organization's performance and growth. The overall tone nevertheless was positive.

The Role of the Interviewer

As a neutral party, I was able to find common ground and agree on productive goals with each person for the coming session. This set me up to play a major role in the success of our meeting because I had a deep understanding of each person *before* he or she entered the room.

The initial contact, even by telephone, was billed as an information-gathering exercise. It was, in fact, first contact. Just as with first impressions, people set their expectations based on it, right or wrong.

The stance of the interviewer is taken to be the stance of the organization. For this reason, it is important to embody the four qualities of professional inquiry, which together bring out the best a person has to offer without compromising their concerns or issues.

The Four Qualities of Professional Inquiry

1. *Professionalism.* The core intent and reason behind the interview is to generate powerful, productive change in a professional endeavor. This means improving the performance of the individuals involved and their collective impact on behalf of the organization. Therefore, at all times, regardless of either levity or anger expressed (and both are okay), the interaction is anchored in the behavior and competence expected of a professional.

2. *Neutrality.* The stance is not one of helping or opposing either side in contentious issues. Instead, it is about finding a way forward that will improve everyone's situation. It should be noted that *neutrality* refers to individual points of view. However, the work is biased toward finding solutions, and that must be explicit at all times.

3. *Compassion.* This means genuine concern for each person involved and his or her emotional experience. Emotion is a legitimate influence in the world of concerns and intents, influencing outcome as well as the process. Listening entails endeavoring to understand what the person is going through and reflect it back to him or her empathetically.

4. *Passion.* Fervor for results, professional contribution, and achievement fuel and improve the quality of individual accomplishment and collaboration. Respond enthusiastically when you hear it in the voice or words of anyone you are interviewing, encouraging them to make the best possible use of it.

Success Rules

- Understanding the territory of change helps you avoid or prepare for challenges, makes it possible to weigh the advantages of options and helps you deal effectively with unplanned interruptions.
- Storylistening, the complement of storytelling, is an effective way to elicit the perspectives of others.
- The Reconnaissance Report is an effective way to synthesize interviews, presenting a snapshot of the change territory. It highlights themes, concerns, educational needs, and opportunities across a group of MVPs.
- The stance of the interviewer is taken to be the stance of the organization by the interviewee. For this reason, it is important to embody professionalism during the interviews.

5

Accelerating Change Through Performance Communities

According to World Bank president Jim Wolfensohn, communities were "the heart and soul" of the bank's Knowledge Management (KM) initiative in the mid-1990s. Inside the bank, we called them *thematic groups*.

When we started the KM initiative, we found five communities inside the organization that had figured out how to survive despite a community-toxic environment—one that was hostile to groups of people getting together outside the hierarchy to discuss what mattered most.

Our team saw the potential in what were then being called *communities of practice*, a new idea that identified the power in groups of people who share a common set of goals. We set about building a community-friendly environment, and within two years the organization had over 120 communities.

People everywhere were advancing KM in the course of their work. Best of all, there was almost complete alignment. This means they thought not so much about KM but about what they wanted to achieve in the context of their own goals. By virtue of the ways communities operate, they pushed forward on thousands of fronts simultaneously, shifting the culture and taking the people along with it. This was a mighty force, accelerating change not just within the organization but also throughout the world because many of the bank's communities crossed the organizational boundary.

Imagine this working for you: a new kind of community in which people work together with colleagues, stakeholders, business partners, and in some cases even competitors to share what they know, achieving results far beyond what any one person can accomplish alone.

These communities work interdependently to advance major initiatives among their own people, addressing specific issues that they are best equipped to understand and resolve.

The learning in these groups takes place in real time, drawing on all levels of experience to take performance and output to extraordinary new levels.

Organizations around the world have been studying just how to do this for decades, with major advances in the past ten years. We are learning how to bring people together and turn them into communities that perform, accelerating the evolution of change. I call these unique groups *performance communities.*

In your imagination, envision a buzzing hive. Hear the hum. Feel the vibration of bees at work. No one is in charge, not even the queen bee. Research on bees shows that in fact she does not direct the workers. Rather, each bee "knows" what to do. They carry out their cooperative tasks based on cues they receive from each other and the environment. Yet the bees work together as if guided by a greater intelligence. Together their efforts culminate in the productivity of the hive. They build the honeycomb and line it with honey at speeds that inspire the imagination.

What a wonder it is to see a project team, a meeting, a committee, or a group of volunteers turn into a beehive. The transformation can be startling. One moment, they are all over the map, moving in random fashion, blocking each other, and coming up with off-the-wall ideas that go in different directions. Then, in a turn of events, as if a hidden conductor stepped in, the group gels into a highly coordinated collaboration. People complement each other in their approaches, playing off each other's strengths and supporting each other's weaknesses like a champion sports team.

COMMUNITY PAST AND PRESENT

Community is how people have always worked and learned together. For thousands of years, we depended on our communities for survival. Our unique capacity to grow and learn was made possible through our relationships to our families, tribes, and villages. In fact, our presence here today is a testimony to the success of our ancestors' communities to deliver on the bottom line: survival.

Although times have changed, community continues to deal strong hands. Technology that reaches around the world brings the best minds available together in virtual communities. New capacities have emerged through collaborative applications.

Communities form all the time inside, outside, and across an organization when business partners, stakeholders, members, and employees work together to develop solutions to problems. They form spontaneously in coffee shops, living rooms, hallways, and boardrooms after the meeting ends. Yet most organizations today do not make use of community. They instead rely on traditional management hierarchies to oversee and get work done. This is one reason that building performance communities can be a strategic advantage.

For a performance community to thrive and generate solid returns, three dimensions must be optimized: business benefits, community concerns, and participant payoffs:

- *Business benefits* refer to the return the sponsoring organization receives. They justify the investment of time, money, and people by providing value in exchange.
- *Community concerns* identify the issues people band together to address. By joining forces, they want to achieve progress on these fronts.

- *Participant payoffs* are rewards each person receives by participating in a community. It may be personal or professional and can be different for each member.

When all three of these are operating in the best possible relation to each other, they act as an exceptional tool for accelerating change. A living social network can achieve results across all three dimensions: business, community, and participants. Each provides value to the other.

THE THREE DIMENSIONS OF SUCCESSFUL PERFORMANCE COMMUNITIES

Business Benefits
These draw organizations to invest in a community. The returns can be substantial and come in a variety of forms — for example:

- Improved operational performance
- Innovation
- Better product and service design, development, delivery
- Increased engagement with stakeholders, including customers or members
- Better skill development through cross-pollination
- Increased client or stakeholder satisfaction
- Improved communications
- Greater market reach

Community Concerns
These are the causes that bring together the members of a community. They are the shared motivation that drives people to collaborate in the first place, joining their efforts on behalf shared objectives — for example:

- Executing a high-value task
- Championing a social cause
- Contributing to a field of expertise

- Receiving group recognition or advancement
- Achieving political objectives

Participant Payoffs
This is the individual level that motivates each person to show up and give his or her best. Since performance communities operate under volunteer principles, the payoffs must be clear, inspiring, and compelling — for example:

- Skill building
- Recognition
- Proximity to power and influence
- Professional advancement
- Problem solving
- Support

Imagine several different kinds of groups with the three dimensions of business benefits, community concerns, and participant payoffs operating in the most favorable ways:

- A tightly knit group of champions meets every Monday morning to update each other and surface issues as they roll out a complex change initiative. Together they identify common problems, develop solutions they will coordinate across the organization, and provide each other with personal and professional support.

  Business benefits: Solution development and coordination of a change rollout

  Community concerns: Cross-support in a difficult, complex job role

  Participant payoffs: Professional advancement and peer networking

- Professional constituencies meet with the CEO and senior management team at biweekly coffees. In a relaxed atmosphere, they share dessert and brainstorm how strategic objectives can gain better traction internally. When they go back to their offices, they talk about their visit "upstairs," batting around ideas with the president. The follow-up conversations with colleagues bring important insights that feed the next coffee with the CEO and spread news organically.

Business benefits: Increased traction for strategy, grassroots communications

Community concerns: Opportunity to influence leadership, access to resources

Participant payoffs: Proximity to power (the CEO), professional visibility

• In the cafeteria every month, technical experts have lunch together and troubleshoot problems that are cropping up in the cracks between their departments. Together they identify issues, generate grassroots solutions, sidestep bureaucracy, and keep their projects on the fast track.

Business benefits: Smoother cross-functional operations and low-cost advanced skill development

Community concerns: Accelerated projects, internal support for a specific role

Participant payoffs: Professional support, peer networking, and access to a brain trust

Each of these is a *performance community*—a group of people highly motivated working toward goals that generate benefits for organizational performance. What makes them function at their best?

Social Learning Systems

Etienne Wenger is best known for his work on communities of practice, groups that share a common practice or application and learn collectively: the appliance repair workers who meet for lunch once a week to share the ins and outs of keeping their machinery running, a cluster of classmates wrestling together over a difficult assignment, or a bunch of biodiversity specialists pooling their experience to improve their understanding.[1]

Wenger's work on communities of practice was groundbreaking. Not surprisingly, he was not alone. A vibrant community of collaborative practitioners has emerged around the globe to take this work forward. One online group, CPsquare, provides a wealth of information including online discussions, explorations of emerging technology, access to members' publications, and calendars of events around the world.[2]

A COMMUNITY OF PRACTICE

Imagine a tightly knit group of general contractors who meet every Saturday evening at the bowling alley to update each other on their trials and tribulations. As they tally their scores and sip sodas, they discuss new building codes, dealing with difficult customers, and how best to sink a concrete pillar in the local soil. They are a community of practice, sharing what they know and developing and refining it so they can succeed in their work.

Wenger has broadened his interest to what he calls social learning systems.[3] He identifies four trends that provide valuable insight into how communities work: horizontalization, partialization, personalization, and individualization. Each provides deep understanding of what makes a performance community operate at its best:

• *Horizontalization.* Learning is normally thought of as vertical, with knowledge passed down from a teacher to a student, who looks up to the instructor for guidance. In this model, the teacher has the know-how and bestows it on a recipient. Horizontal learning, by contrast, happens among partners who are in it together. Instead of being given from teacher to student download, it is a peer-to-peer exchange. There is an equality and give-and-take.

• *Partialization.* Today each person's knowledge and expertise is part of a larger puzzle. It is no longer possible for one person to hold the entire body of expertise in a given area. Instead, experts possess a portion of know-how that is part of the field. Everyone and every organization is part of a system. We exist in relationship with the other members of our systems. In this sense, we hold an increasingly partial segment of the whole.

• *Personalization.* Wenger says, "Creativity is a voluntary act of engagement with a problem, which cannot be designed or prescribed in the way that a routine action can."[4] This means that a person has to want to be involved in order to marshal her total engagement and bring all of her creative resources to bear on a particular issue. Participation and motivation play increasingly important roles, rather than coercion or compliance. Today it becomes increasingly important to understand what motivates people to participate and enroll them to participate with enthusiasm.

• *Individualization.* For over 100,000 years, people were born, grew up, paired off, raised children, lived, and died in a single community. Only in the past few thousand years have we begin to spend portions of our lives in different communities. Today many of us enter and leave anywhere from twenty to one hundred communities every day. We participate in unique groups that include home, work, after-work, school, electronic lists, project teams, social media, and many more. As a result, we are becoming more and more unique.

These trends help us to shift our approach from a traditional team orientation to a more organic and natural way of understanding how people learn and perform together. They show why social networking and social software are so attractive and light the way toward understanding how to use communities to get change right.

For example, I belong to a group of people who have been actively involved in experimental theater, enjoy solo wilderness camping, lead organizational change initiatives, have extensive experience working with CEOs, and have more than thirty years of experience performing as a storyteller. This makes me somewhat unique—but no more unique than you. You have your own constellation of experience that distinguishes your background, experience, and know-how.

ETIENNE WENGER ON COMMUNITIES OF PRACTICE

Etienne Wenger is widely recognized as a pioneer and leading thinker in the field of organizational community. He was one of the first to use the term *community of practice* to refer to groups of people who together accumulate and share their collective learning. A book that Wenger coauthored, *Cultivating Communities of Practice,* is a guide describing the ups, the downs, and the how-tos for developing these groups in organizations.[5]

Being engaged to the fullest of one's identity is the source of creativity required for participation in a knowledge economy. The engagement of identity, if you will, replaces the whip of the early industrial model. In the industrial model, you told people, "Forget your identity. Leave it at the door! Leave your sense of meaningfulness at the door. Instead, do what I tell you to do. Then, when you are done, you may go back, put your identity back on, go into the world, and do whatever you want." That's the industrial model. In the new model, you can't do that, because the identity you want people to leave at the door is precisely the resource they have to be creative.

We are fundamentally social beings. Our participation in human practices is how we become who we are. Learning in the context of engagement, identity and innovation of communities starts within our

Expert Input

little family and then moves into broader and broader circles . . . In this sense, the whole notion of social practice is fundamental.

Communities of practice are flourishing because they provide support for this kind of learning. They are an expression of their members' will to make them exist . . . They are not driven by institutional fiat. They are more in line with these more subtle forms of identity that derive from engagement with the world and engagement with peers and others. To provide anchors for identity is still very important. It is not that the issue of identity is disappearing. On the contrary, it is becoming more intense a concern than in the past. But what serves people's identity is no longer simply providing affiliation and information . . . Information is now a commodity. To be a source of information does not provide something unique. What provides something really unique is the ability to interact with interesting groups of people that mean a lot to you. People do not want to have the identity of an association. They want to experience their identity as professionals engaged in meaningful learning, alive in knowledge creation.

Source: Kahan, S. "Engagement, Identity, and Innovation: Etienne Wenger on Communities of Practice." *Journal of Association Leadership,* Winter 2004.

Implications for Performance Communities

The ideal business performance community balances horizontal learning and vertical learning. Vertical learning is bringing in the thought leaders, the exemplars. Horizontal learning happens when people have the chance to self-organize, as they would on a break at a conference or in a coffee shop.

THREE WAYS TO BALANCE VERTICAL AND HORIZONTAL LEARNING

---

1. *Combine vertical and horizontal learning.* Provide a presentation by the leading expert, and follow it with a loosely organized conversation in a business casual environment, like a living room or bar.

2. *Hold multiple events, each with a focus on one or the other.* At one session, provide an intensive learning event that exposes people to the thought leaders, giving the authority the stage and providing support materials and case studies that showcase his or her materials. Then host a peer-to-peer exchange with the express purpose of allowing people to work together to address common challenges.

3. *Bring in a facilitator to design and lead a self-organizing process,* such as Open Space, World Café, Appreciative Inquiry, or Future Search.* These structures naturally surface opportunities for leaders to emerge (though who emerges as a leader may surprise you) as well as people to work peer-to-peer.

*A number of group processes are designed to help groups self-organize. More information on some of these, including instructions on how to lead them, can be found at http://openspaceworld.com/, http://www.theworldcafe.com/ http://appreciativeinquiry.case.edu/, and http://www.futuresearch.net/

Partialization says that everyone has a part of the puzzle; nobody owns the whole thing. Therefore, it is important to find ways to include those with varying amounts of time or effort to give. If you limit participation to those who have a lot of time or energy, you may miss important contributions. This leads to a value-based model of participation, rather than one that is time based or effort based. In other words, what is important in a performance community is the value generated, not the amount of time or effort expended.

Lest we become fanatical about visible displays of participation, this is a good place to point out the value of lurking and the valid continuum on which people transit from passive to active participation. This phenomenon, called *legitimate peripheral participation*, has been well documented.[6]

When people join a group, they often achieve member status in a community by engaging in low-risk activities that further the group's goals. Through these tasks, they become acquainted with the work, terms, mores, taboos, and ways of the community. Some people prefer this type of participation. It is no less valuable than other more obvious forms of contribution. A strong performance community will have multiple ways for members to participate, presenting a wide choice of both effort and visibility.

Performance communities meet people where they are and draw them into greater participation by providing real value. This makes it possible for people to self-select their point of contribution based on personal preference and style with regard to time, effort, and visibility. The amount of time and effort people have to give to their performance community varies widely and is often independent of the amount of value they generate or receive.

The Value-Based Contribution Current

It is the value, then, that generates the pull, not the time spent or energy contributed. A healthy community creates a current that pulls people along, encouraging and enabling them to create greater and greater value. Because value flows both ways, enriching the giver as well as the recipient, this current also increases the value received. This is a great dynamic! The more people give, the more they get, thanks to the current.

Just as Figure 5.1 shows, this current pulls people from less to more value independent of the amount of effort, time, or visibility they have. It is all based on value.

This is important when in the process of getting change right, because it makes clear that simply having a lot of time, putting in extra effort, or carrying high visibility does not guarantee increased contribution. Rather, the value that is generated for the change effort, the community, and the participants is the true indicator of positive impact.

In other words, don't measure a community's performance by how often it meets; how much time is spent building its database, putting together its documentation, or building its Web site; or even by how much they are seen by others. Instead, turn your attention toward the business benefits, community concerns, and participant payoffs. This is where *the value is identified and can be tracked.*

FIGURE 5.1 The Value-Based Contribution Current

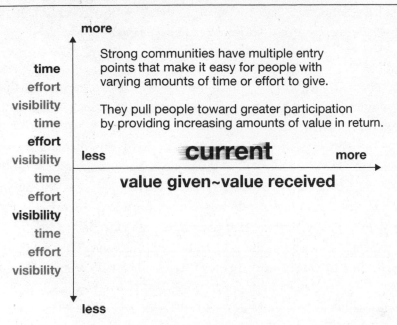

Measuring Business Value

Business benefits are owned by the sponsoring organization. They are the justification for the investment of time, money, and people in the performance community. The organization providing these resources is the sponsor of the performance community. The clearer the arrangement between the sponsor and the performance community is, the easier it is to understand the value exchange.

I once led a project in which the change office in headquarters decided to fund a performance community in the field. The business benefit was to make local progress on the global change initiative. In return, headquarters provided money so the members could obtain resources that included consultants and training. A project plan was developed that showed milestones the performance community took responsibility for. As long as the project was on track, money flowed.

Metrics should be developed jointly with members of the performance community. They lay out what needs to be accomplished, and the resulting resources that will be made available.

Cultivating Community Value

Members determine the community's concerns, representing their combined interests and goals. This is where the value resides at the community level.

The concerns of the World Bank's Highways Thematic Group included everything from the deterioration of asphalt in high humidity to the development of intelligent policy for using roads to enhance economic development, and everything in between. For this community to be happy, healthy, and productive, they needed to be sharing experience, know-how, and information on highways. They wanted to see the impact of their work on knowledge in their field. Very little could come between them and these activities, or they would quickly become concerned that their community was deteriorating.

Value given and value received is measured internally in a community by the ability to carry out shared concerns. Creating a community mandate is an excellent way to cultivate the community's concerns, generating value for the group:

Guidelines for Creating and Using Community Mandates

- *Create a statement of purpose, a mission, an agenda, or a set of goals tied directly to the community's concerns.* These are all effective forms of a community mandate. The process of creating the mandate is an exercise in itself. Valuable issues will be raised, such as, Who is in and who is out? What constitutes progress? What are the limits of our reach?
- *Anchor all activities specified in the document in the community's concerns.* For example, it is not enough to specify, "Build a Web site." The value of the Web site needs to be primary (that is, more important than the site itself). Instead, the activity should be specified in this way: "We will build the relationships among

our members, improving our capacity to share what we know and contribute to the field. This includes the development of a Web site that will provide a directory to all of our members as well as an initial document repository for papers past and present."

- *Use the community mandate as a tool.* Turn to it to periodically evaluate progress and raise issues of innovation, new circumstances, trends, and expanded or contracted scope.

Providing Participant Value

Wenger's ideas of personalization and individualization help us to see both how important it is to appeal to each person's motivation for participation and how truly unique every member is. This presents a challenge in a hands-off environment, but communities are hands-on and built through relationships among real people. All participants assess the value they receive in ways unique to their needs and changing circumstances.

This is why it is important that someone in the community be in touch with participants: engaging in conversation, opening up the door to new ideas and new ways of generating individual value, and harvesting the unique experience of the members.

CONVERSATION STARTERS TO ENGAGE PARTICIPANTS IN GENERATING VALUE

- Why do you participate?
- Are there specific goals or rewards you intend to reap through your participation?
- Have you received any unexpected rewards from your participation?
- What are you most interested in contributing?
- What would you practically like to get from this group?

- What is the most extraordinary result you could hope to glean from the group?
- Is there a particular person or group of people you would like to engage more deeply?
- Is anyone missing from this group?
- Are there activities that we could be doing that you would find more rewarding?
- How can you upgrade the rewards you are getting from your participation? Can this be done with less effort or time commitment on your part?

Building a Performance Community

In the course of building performance communities, management tasks change from supervising subordinates to enabling colleagues. To bring the know-how that communities create to bear on organizational needs, managers need to cultivate relationships built on trust and healthy growth. Here are ten techniques that embrace this way of working and give guidance on how to build communities that perform:

1. *Share the idea with everyone who has a stake in success.* This is like a mini-list of your MVPs but for this performance community. Let's say that you want to start performance communities to address issues unique to Africa, Western Europe, and the Pacific Rim. Ask yourself, Who has a stake in our success in these regions? Whose interest is already aligned with their success as regions? Approach these people, and tell them you are intending to form a community. Listen to their responses, and take them to heart as you go forward.

2. *Interact with potential members.* Get out of your office, and meet with those who may join. Talk to them on the telephone. Send them personal e-mails. Ask for ideas, suggestions, and the names of others who would benefit by taking part. Listen to understand their perspective and concerns, especially if they are different from your own. You may be able to identify new participant payoffs. Embrace multiple perspectives as long as everyone is working toward the same community concerns.

3. *Identify a social architect.* A social architect, someone who understands and facilitates the interactions among members, is one of the two most important roles in a performance community (the other is the resident expert, listed next). This should be a "people person" with strong interpersonal communication skills and a genuine desire to help the community succeed. Responsibilities include

- Identifying important issues as they arise
- Planning and facilitating events
- Linking members of the performance community
- Fostering professional development
- Coordinating development of learning tools: documents, Web sites, and events, for example
- Cultivating the health of the performance community: making sure people are getting what they need, results are being achieved, and the tasks taken on match the resources available

4. *Identify resident experts.* This is the second most important role (after the social architects) in your performance community. Resident experts have deep knowledge in the community's domain. They are sources of guidance for group decisions and will attract others to participate. They wield their authority through know-how and experience rather than by decree.

5. *Invite people to participate.* Communicate to people through their preferred media. If they are telephone people, call them. If they are e-mail people, write them. If they read *Discovery* magazine, put an ad in it. In your invitation, be clear about business benefits, community concerns, and participant payoffs. Tell them what you are hoping to accomplish, and ask them to be part of the effort.

6. *Make it easy for members to contact each other.* As soon as the performance community forms, publish a directory with phone numbers and e-mail addresses. You may wish to include a section in the directory that members fill in any way they want. Personal information should not be frowned on. "I like to sail and have three grandkids," for example, increases rapport with colleagues. The same is true for requests for assistance. "I need help with the Nigeria project," for example, facilitates transactions within the community.

7. *Invite open discussions.* Allow divergent ideas; don't push consensus. If small groups form in your performance community to champion alternative perspectives, help them explore these. This multiplicity of perspective bolsters the work. Tackling issues from many sides is one of the strengths of a community. As long as people are focused on the shared concerns of the community, differing perspectives strengthen their abilities.

8. *Communicate, communicate, and communicate!* Do everything you can to keep people in the loop. It's no coincidence that *community* and *communication* have the same root. Come to know your community's preferred types of communication media, and use them. There will probably be several. You may need brown bag lunches, one-on-one meetings among core members, e-mails and electronic lists. Do whatever works. Construct communiqués so that they invite participation. For example, rather than provide exhaustive minutes, highlight main points and invite others to fill in gaps. Have the members take responsibility for the communication.

9. *Stay open to continued suggestions.* Performance communities evolve, and this is normal. A community is a living thing and changes over time.

Create ways for new ideas to be reviewed and processed easily without derailing progress.

10. *Develop presentation tool kits.* Make it easy for members to share their work with colleagues and other interested people. You may wish to assist them in developing PowerPoint presentations, brochures, CDs, or product samples. These tool kits support your group's success. Each member will reach into his or her social network to support and endorse the work they are doing. Tool kits make that easier.

Ramping Up Performance Communities

A performance community that takes off is something to treasure. People work together in an esprit de corps that enhances each person's contribution. The group achieves far more than the sum of its participants, yielding multiples of productivity. It becomes easier for everyone to get what he or she comes for.

Not all groups achieve this, of course. Some will say, "That doesn't happen here. We don't do the kumbaya thing." They mistakenly think of community as holding hands and hugging. But this is a limited view of the power of people to collaborate. Performance communities are about *performance.* When they shift to a new level of delivery, the results are stunning and obvious.

Community cannot be mandated. If the boss walks in and demands, "Everybody collaborate!" it is not a given that a community will perform. However, performance communities can be deliberately stimulated to achieve great leaps in performance:

Let Every Participant Know He or She Is Valued, and Be Specific

By explicitly identifying a person's achievements, contributions, talent, and relevant experience, you invoke her participation in these areas while at the same time alerting other members of the community to the value they can generate through interaction. Do not do this by asking the person to talk about herself. It is genuinely difficult to articulate this on behalf of yourself. It puts most people in a position that feels awkward because they confuse it with self-aggrandizement. Instead, take the initiative and highlight the relevant material for them. In addition, people who are treated with respect and welcomed engage more freely. Make it known to each person why he or she is valued. Be explicit. Here are three ways to do this:

- *Make a public statement at a community meeting.* This can be done in a couple of minutes, as during a round of introductions, or in more detail when a particular task would benefit, as in discussing a high-priority challenge that a particular member is exceptionally qualified to address.
- *Document members' experience in a directory of expertise.* This is a database that makes visible the expert skill and knowledge of members. A project team created this for the entire World Bank, pulling together professional credentials, training, and experience. It also included a place for people to enter anything they deemed appropriate. It was fully searchable, posted on the Web, and linked to all document attributions.
- Hold receptions in which participants are sought out and recognized for their professional contributions, especially when they are part of the community's mandate.

Frequently Summarize, Support, and Challenge the Community in the Context of Business Goals

This three-step process has a strong effect on community performance, injecting great force into productivity:

- *Summarize* the context, review progress, changing circumstances, and the potential to make a difference with the business goals.
- *Support* the community by recognizing its strengths, achievements, and the unique circumstances and talent of the members, and use those to the greatest advantage.

- *Challenge* the group to raise the bar on its performance. Identify specific areas where excellence can be achieved and improvement can have significant consequences.

It works most powerfully when the person who delivers this material is someone the community trusts deeply and knows the community and its members well. This person is then put in a position to wield the trust he or she is given and use it to great effect. His intimate knowledge of the community members will help him to customize the process to rouse the members individually and collectively. The more frequently this is done—and it can be done up to weekly—the more powerful the results can be. You must of course take into consideration how often the performance community meets.

Create Opportunities for Members of the Community to Address Organizational Leadership

Speaking to leadership is extremely valuable to members and the community. It provides professional visibility, generates a visceral sense of contribution, and accelerates impact by the community and the larger organization. These sessions can be short, perhaps as an addition to an otherwise dedicated agenda, or longer, as in stand-alone presentations. They must be related to leaders' current concerns for maximum impact. Here are three suggestions for how to make this happen:

- *Design a presentation* around the performance community's contribution to the change effort. Have a moderator who understands the value the community has generated and facilitates their interaction with the leadership.
- *Establish a theme* that is a hot topic among leadership, and provide the community's perspective on it, sticking to topics that appeal to the self-interest of the leaders.
- *Volunteer the community's efforts to lead an interactive session* that addresses emergent issues of great concern. Showcase the community as a proactive agent of change in the organization.

Success Rules

- Performance communities operate at peak performance when they optimize the value they generate for business benefits, community concerns, and participant payoffs.
- Four trends in social learning—horizontalization, partialization, personalization, and individualization—illustrate how to use communities to get change right.
- The amount of time and effort people have to give to their performance community varies widely and is often independent of the amount of value they generate or receive. Strong communities have multiple entry points and pull people toward greater participation by providing increasing amounts of value.
- Building performance communities requires a different way of looking at management. The task changes from supervising subordinates to enabling colleagues.
- Performance communities can be deliberately stimulated to achieve extraordinary results.

Generating Dramatic Surges in Progress

The original touchstone was basanite, a smooth, black stone used to test the quality of gold and silver. It was rubbed across the precious metal, and the authenticity could be determined by the color of the streak produced. The word *touchstone* now means anything that tests genuineness or excellence.

Genuineness and excellence are at the heart of what drives people forward in dramatic surges of progress. They are the roots. From this powerful core, real transformation takes place. But people will want to test it. So give them something powerful to test.

For this very reason I created *Touchstone Events.* These are gatherings that dive deep and make contact with what is real, essential, and core to the work of change in ways that generate sudden, striking forward momentum. The purpose of a Touchstone Event is to gain a perch in a particular culture by striking a keynote, like a tuning fork, that causes the entire community to resonate in response with powerful authenticity. Done well, a Touchstone Event moves the entire community forward in one giant leap, constructing the common beliefs and understandings that sustain coherent activity into the foreseeable future.

In the mid-1990s the internal perception was that the World Bank was a cold and uncaring institution, populated by the educational elite who operated on poverty from a distance. Headquarters lacked warmth too. With over ten thousand people in a half-dozen buildings in downtown Washington, D.C., it was easy to feel lost among strangers—perhaps even more so because the cultural diversity was so great and the ethnicity so varied that no one culture dominated the population. Many were concerned about this lack of community. This included the president, Jim Wolfensohn, and his internal communications team, of which I was a member.

When I was interviewed for my job, I was asked what I could offer to help create an esprit de corps among all staff. There were open discussions about bringing people together and creating greater camaraderie. I was asked to use my background in street theater to create a special brand of gathering that would be customized to the World Bank culture, assembling thousands in a face-to-face experience that would enhance everyone's professionalism.

Between 1978 and 1989, I had produced and performed street theater. In my work I brought together actors, dancers, musicians, and poets, both professional and amateur, to improvise performance art in public spaces. I led two troupes during that time and delivered a series of original one-man shows. My goal was to create live events that stopped busy people, caught their attention in irresistible ways, and compelled them to participate.

My capacity to involve people, to engage them in compelling ways, would now be put to use inside an organization. Little did I imagine the first large-scale gathering of World Bank staff I would produce.

During the attacks of September 11, 2001, our small internal communications team coordinated the World Bank's internal response. We could see the smoke billowing from the crash into the Pentagon from a window across the hallway. Separating rumors from the chaos in communications that ensued was a challenge. The Internet, jammed and overloaded, failed to download newscasts in a timely fashion.

Our unit was new, and we had not yet installed our television sets to monitor world events. My wife, Laura, at home, held our telephone to the television screen so I could hear what was being broadcast.

We liaised with the Department of Treasury, responsible for coordinating emergency response in downtown D.C., and The World Bank's president's office. Before noon, we made the decision to close our offices. As the director of communications dictated to me, I typed the message to all Bank staff members to evacuate headquarters.

Along with the rest of the nation and the world, we struggled to figure out how to respond appropriately even though we lacked enough information to know what was really happening. Early the next morning, with everyone stunned and grief-stricken, our team went into huddle and decided that in forty-eight hours, on Friday, September 14, we would have an all-staff gathering.

The purpose was to bring people together, reminding them of the community they belonged to in a time of anguish. We would openly acknowledge the grief in our hearts, giving it a home inside the organization. We were doing our best to set our sights on the uncertain, difficult road toward healing and the new world we were tumbling into.

On September 14, with short notice, we brought about two thousand people into our atrium for a twenty-minute gathering. By Wolfensohn's request, we had live music, Bach's Suite for Solo Cello No. 1 in G-Major, Sarabande, a powerfully moving piece that is introspective, complex, and emotionally intimate.

Wolfensohn characteristically delivered his words straight from the heart. He asked staff members to join hands, which had never been done before. Then he asked for a minute of silence in remembrance. Open weeping could be heard in the large, silent atrium. The event was as quiet as it was profound—and a marked departure from the dispassionate and efficient communications of the past.

In the weeks that followed, a series of activities aimed to establish a new, more humane ambience inside the organization. A memorandum from the president encouraged staff members to travel only if they felt safe. Vice presidents and directors walked the hallways, checking in with staff and engaging in personal conversations to see how people were doing. Clinics were set up for counseling. Special events were hosted to educate people on Islam. Security staff members were made available to chaperone people on request. Leadership responded to the tragedy by turning toward other people instead of away from them. Months passed. Stability returned.

Throughout the next year and a half, we brought people together in the atrium to celebrate the work of our support staff, explore innovation together, and review the year with all its ups and downs. The atrium became a place for our community to assemble. We pumped the events out to thousands in the field through the Internet. We even ate together, serving cake, ice cream, and juice on occasion.

By the end of 2002 we were ready to venture into new territory. A small group of us set up the World Bank's Celebration of Cultures, a fifty-minute performance in the headquarters atrium by staff for staff. Held in December, it was meant to be a nonsectarian event that roused the spirit, extolling and paying tribute to our diversity.

We invited World Bank staff members and their families to take the stage, performing music, dance, poetry, and other expressions of cultural heritage. To ensure no one would be left out, a series of pre-events took place months prior that allowed everyone, without exception, to perform. From these events, presentations were selected for the final extravaganza.

The culmination event presented the best performances the World Bank had to offer. Among the performers was President Wolfensohn as well as employees from every part of the organization and their spouses, children, and grandchildren. This internal event spanned the globe with distance participants joining by Internet and satellite.

We had whole neighborhoods onstage folk dancing, young children playing jazz solos, models parading emerging fashions from around the world, belly dancers, innovative clothing stitched by Bank employees, and even devotional hymns that filled the twelve-story atrium with voices of beauty singing praise in many languages.

Over the course of the fifteen months between September 2001 and December 2002, the World Bank had found a way forward that was heartfelt, acknowledging the suffering of tremendous tragedy and generating a shift in the internal culture toward warmth and unity.

From this point forward, I began my work producing face-to-face events to advance change initiatives that drew on the best that people had to offer, channeling their hope and professional passions into getting change right.

This chapter describes how such events have been used to advance better well and reservoir care to improve oil and gas production in an international energy company.

Designing Touchstone Events That Move Professionals

Being the meaning-making creatures we are, we create a great deal of interpretation around high-intensity activities, from traumas and life-changing transitions to exciting breakthroughs.

For our personal lives, life-changing transitions include the shift from childhood to adulthood, marriage, and the arrival of children. An exciting breakthrough might be a new job that represents significant advancement, or a great success in the marketplace that wins accolades and offers new opportunities. Traumas are deeply distressing or disturbing experiences and need to be addressed, enabling grieving and finding the best path forward.

For our professional lives, there are equivalents. When these are properly executed, they bond professionals together in the pursuit of common goals, making possible a great deal of coordinated activity and progress and raising all boats with the tide. The impact of these orchestrated events is carried forward in powerful and broad behavior changes executed en masse. The results can carry everyone forward on wave after wave of progress.

Touchstone Events are professional rites of passage—special gatherings that shift a community from one state of performance to an more advanced, irrevocably advancing their status.[1] Because rites of passage must be grounded in a community's beliefs, values, and social hierarchy, they require great sensitivity to the nuances and needs of a particular population.

The usual conference antics, ranging from rock bands and laser light shows to M&M-throwing facilitators, create a carnival atmosphere that pales in comparison to a Touchstone Event. It is like contrasting a ride on a Ferris wheel at a local circus with a well-crafted wedding ceremony. The first is fun on a good day and a nice diversion; the latter is a life-affirming milestone that changes the participants forever in the ongoing human drama of existence.

Most organizations sadly miss the opportunity that bringing together their prized professionals offers and create something that at best is a nice memory. To avoid this, apply strategic event production to create dramatic surges in change work. It combines two important ends with power and binding impact: (1) integration and adjustment to changing circumstances and (2) execution of a bold vision.

TOUCHSTONE EVENTS: THE JET ENGINES OF CHANGE

Jet engines generate tremendous thrust. Here is how they work:

1. They suck in air at the front with a fan.
2. A compressor raises the pressure of the air. The compressor is made up of fans with many blades and attached to a shaft. The blades work together to uniformly compress the air.
3. The compressed air is sprayed with fuel.
4. A spark ignites the mixture.
5. The burning gases expand and blast out through the nozzle, at the back of the engine. As the jets of gas shoot backward, the engine and the aircraft are thrust forward.

Here's how Touchstone Events generate their thrust:

1. They draw people and resources in to prepare for an event, just like a good party. When you communicate the intentions of the gathering, people begin to anticipate the opportunity and forward momentum, and they become engaged.

2. As the event nears, people begin to sense more acutely what is at stake and the opportunities presented. This anticipation across all the parties raises their participation, creating uniform pressure across all contributors.

3. Contributors to the event are given coaching and guidance on how to realize progress and make forward advances in the heat of the live event, making them more likely to catch fire with passion and possibility.

4. The event takes place. Good intentions are transformed into action, harvesting the preparation and generating forward movement across many streams of activity simultaneously.

5. The good ideas catch and move through the participants, generating chain reactions of interactions. The focus of the Touchstone Event provides the channel through which all this force travels, thrusting the change program forward.

Guidelines for Creating Touchstone Events

To create an exceptional event that brings people together and moves them forward collectively, you need to follow important guidelines.

1. *Know and engage your audience.* Some people will not be in a receptive mood for reasons beyond your control. Perhaps they aren't feeling well or they quarreled with their spouse on the way over. They should not distract your focus. Others are coming to cheerlead you. They will support your work regardless. The event is not for them either. There is a third group: they have come to see if there is something exceptional here. They are inquiring, ready, open-minded, and responsive. They are your primary audience. Engage them, speak to their aspirations, and clearly show them what is possible. Articulate your direction in ways that enable easy and accurate understanding. Arouse their desire to be part of something special and grand.

2. *Embrace current perceptions.* Don't fight prevailing winds. Rather, sail into them, and use them to chart new directions. Too often events are created that fly in the face of common understanding and as a result seem artificial, self-serving, or manipulative. The power in assembly is in its authenticity. Don't be afraid of what is. Use it to propel you and your colleagues into a better future.

3. *Spring from the current state to a new one.* If the mood is dark, don't pretend it is otherwise. Instead capitalize on the depth of feeling, and use it to move you to courageous action. If perceptions are scattered, create an opportunity to focus them. When enthusiasm is high, ramp it up. Regardless of perceptions, you can use them to raise the bar on performance.

4. *Open with a compelling attention grabber.* Don't start with long lists of appreciation or the obligatory acknowledgment of authorities. The audience will judge the nature of the event in the first minute, so open with something forceful and interesting—your hook. Give people a palpable sense of the magic of the moment, the reason for calling them together.

5. *Tell your story.* The event is a pivot point, the juncture between two worlds. It is a leadership moment. Help people understand the story they are participating in. Tell what has come before, and show where you are going.

6. *Place your audience in the story.* Make it clear why those in attendance are important. Underline their contribution to success. Celebrate their accomplishments. Acknowledge their struggles. Make them the central characters. The purpose of the event is to catalyze their activity, so give them center stage.

7. *Show what is possible.* Inspire people with the future as it touches the present. Bring the realization of success to life through all of the senses: movement, sound, sight, smell, and taste. Create a multisensory experience that paves the way into a new and better world.

8. *Pick your strong points, and articulate them clearly.* To build a strong impression, be succinct. Pick your main points, and express them with brevity, force, and clarity. Short and powerful rules the moment and wins the hearts.

9. *Convey the emotion of the moment.* People are emotional creatures. Though we have a love affair with logic, it is emotion that moves us. Find the right way to express emotion in your culture, and give it play.

10. *Close with impact.* The last thing people hear or see is what they remember. Make it memorable, easy to understand, significant, and strong.

A Touchstone Event for a Global Energy Company

In 2007–2008 I worked one-on-one with the change leader of a $20 million program to increase the quality of well and reservoir operations for a large energy company. My job was to provide strategic reflection to this leader so he could increase his effectiveness day-to-day in a large, complex initiative that covered the Americas as part of a worldwide effort.

I worked with senior staff in the global enterprise headquarters, helping them to engage professionals across the world effectively. I also worked directly with operational managers and their teams, contributing to their capacity to lead change on the ground in the fields.

After a year of groundwork, we decided it was necessary to pull people from around the world together to advance the Americas initiative. Working collaboratively with headquarters, we identified sixty people to participate in a two-day event. Unlike the World Bank events, this was 100 percent participation. Different culture, different needs.

The vice presidents of operations, technology, and the Americas regions came to participate for the full two days. We did this because their culture demanded it. Engineers are practical, if nothing else, and including the head brass in these activities demonstrated the seriousness of the event.

The recognized thought leaders in each of the primary areas that would make or break the initiative also came. They included technology specialists with deep understanding of the new applications, as well as old hands who understand the wells and reservoirs from decades of on-the-ground experience.

Before the event, we identified which oil platforms and gas fields would be early adopters and brought in their best and brightest staff, including the operational supervisors with high-level understanding of the histories, needs, and care of each location. These were our MVPs. All in one place at one time. The change effort was a $20 million investment, and we were serious about the ROI. This drove the ambition, the scheduling, and the intensity of the gathering.

The first day we engaged people, showing them what was possible, laying out our intentions, holding educational sessions that covered the new methods, mining the collective intelligence of the group, and addressing their concerns.

The second day we made it possible for everyone to design the way forward. Since we were working with engineers, we asked them to identify issues, create time lines, allocate responsibility and resources, and assemble it all on a giant wall chart table.

The event was custom-designed to fit snugly within the culture of their organization, advancing the change initiative aggressively through a face-to-face encounter that drew on the passions of engineers in the oil and gas industry. In two days, we did what otherwise would have easily taken over a year: pulling everyone together to self-organize a dramatic surge forward.

Truthfully, the giant wall-sized chart was an artifact. It was necessary only in that it made progress possible, just as the presence of the vice presidents did. These were cues and methods that made sense in this culture.

Features of Successful Touchstone Events

The purpose of Touchstone Events is to gain a perch in a unique culture and move the entire community forward in one giant leap, constructing the common understanding that will sustain activity in the foreseeable future.

Successful Touchstone Events have three important features:

- *They are a natural extension of the culture in which they arise.* They do not seem like an alien, imposed, or artificial experience. Instead they magnify and amplify emerging trends and new and better way of doing things: the change initiative. They incorporate present-day circumstances and news, encouraging new information to surface, becoming visible and useful.
- *They are a natural conclusion to the work that came before.* Rather than seeming contrived, they make sense in the context of previous circumstances. The fit is natural. Just as a marriage or a graduation is the natural capstone to a sequence of activity, taking it to another level of public support, a Touchstone Event is a way to recognize that something new has arisen and is being endorsed as the next logical step.
- *They accelerate forward progress.* They bring activities to their natural consequences in rapid fashion. Bringing people together, planning and coordinating in advance, and setting the stage for confluence tie up many loose ends simultaneously and accelerate achievements. This results in a jet-power surge forward.

LESLEY SHNEIER ON THE WORLD BANK'S KNOWLEDGE FAIRS

Lesley Shneier is a senior knowledge and learning specialist at the World Bank Group. She comes from South Africa, with a background in social work, human resources, organization change, and management consulting. Lesley has worked at the World Bank in Washington, D.C., since 1985. She was an original member of the World Bank's Knowledge Management team and provided critical skills that made its early work an international success.

One of her most powerful contributions was the World Bank's Knowledge Fairs. She came up with the idea and almost single-handedly; produced the first, which brought together hundreds of practitioners; made knowledge management visible through real-life examples that people could investigate and learn from on their own; and received acclaim from President Wolfensohn as well as those who attended and learned from it.

Our fair included booths that showcased networks of mayors from Central American cities working together on urban renewal, collaborations between World Bank and nongovernmental organizations on biodiversity, and the live demonstration of electronic directories showcasing employees' professional expertise.

This conversation is taken from an interaction that includes Steve Denning, the former program director of knowledge management at the World Bank.

The Knowledge Fair we conducted at the World Bank was quite spectacular. It moved our whole initiative from under the radar to out in the world where everyone could see and touch it.

Lesley: Steve told me to provide training, and I kept saying, "Nobody will go to training unless they know what we are talking about. We need to show them. Let's have an open house. Since we don't have a house, let's use the atrium." No one in the World Bank had ever used our atrium for such an event before that time.

Steve: Lesley, you were passionate about it. It was certainly in conflict with the culture of the World Bank to have a fair. It had never been done before. But you were passionate about it, and I thought, let's do it.

Lesley: Our first Knowledge Fair was in March 1998. Wolfensohn loved what we did and asked us to do it again at the annual meetings. There we had fifty booths. Two were the International Monetary Fund, and the rest were World Bank. We made it thematic. The audience was now external. It included clients, the private sector, heads of central banks, and so on. We created neighborhoods— clusters of booths organized by theme. We were also in the midst of the Asian crisis, so we had quite a lot on that.

We were received well from people outside the Bank.

Lesley: Somebody wrote to Wolfensohn and said he learned more on our floor in two hours than in twenty years of attending annual meetings.

Steve: The Knowledge Fair embodied the image of what this whole thing was about. It crystallized the idea that this was a core thing. There was an image developed that this could be useful.

Lesley: I insisted that it not be demos. I wanted it to be live, in real time, so people could go back to their desks and do what they had seen. They could get questions answered; they could join a thematic group.

They could take action immediately.

Lesley: Yes. They could go back to their offices and do things immediately.

How to Create Touchstone Events with Extraordinary Thrust

When I began designing Touchstone Events, I was confronted by three kinds of people who made the going hard: (1) those who focused primarily on logistics, (2) those who had earned their stripes planning traditional meetings, and (3) those who design the event with a business mind-set.

What has been making people laugh and cry for centuries? The theater. Does the playwright ask the facility staff what can and cannot be done? Does the director? You need a different mind-set if you want to execute a life-changing occasion.

Here are the nine steps to take to bring your Touchstone Event to life:

1. *Customize the event to your audience.* Don't build a generic event. Don't design it for the powers that be. They will be oh so happy when your event carries people away and results in an extraordinary leap in performance. Keep your eye on the ball. This event is for your MVPs—no one else.

2. *Create a great name.* Don't call it the "Enterprise Transformation Summit." Appeal to human interest. Try something like "The Future Is Already Here" or "A Revolution in the Making."

3. *Make the opening compelling and powerful.* Your audience will decide in seconds whether this event is worth their attention. Personalize it, and cut straight to the most exciting thing you have to offer. Don't start with congratulations, acknowledgments, or appreciations. You can work those in later. Knock people's socks off in the first minute.

4. *Provide real value as soon as possible.* Deliver something that makes a difference in people's lives immediately after the opening. Address their most pressing concern. Change their lives for the better.

5. *Don't point people toward some other resource.* Don't say, "Go to our Web site," or "Read this document." Give people real meat to chew on, and they'll go looking for the support materials.

6. *Call people to action.* Tell them what you want them to do, and invite them to start now. The more important the audience, the more critical it is that you follow up with them immediately after the event. (See "Catching People When They Are Ripe" later in this chapter.)

7. *Hit several fronts at once.* Demonstrate that your message is multidimensional by connecting the dots for people in all the important areas of impact. You want people to look around and say, *Holy cow! This stuff is everywhere! This must be the future.*

8. *Engage the audience's peers in planning, delivery, and follow-up.* It's always better to have a message delivered by a regular guy—someone your audience knows and trusts. Don't worry about polish or professional delivery. This is about authenticity, not spin. Show it.

9. *Go out with a bang.* State your core message in an unforgettable delivery. Make it easy for people to answer their friends when they ask, "So what was that all about anyway?"

Grabbing Attention and Keeping It

From producing and performing street theater for decades, I learned what it takes to grab and hold someone's attention when they are on their way somewhere else. You have to go straight to the gut, then give their heads something to think about, and finally deliver the heart. This can all be done in seconds. Here's how.

Grab the Gut

Provide something that is compelling enough to catch the attention of your audience. This means syncing your message with their experience. They should respond quickly and positively but also be able to quickly categorize you as safe, interesting, and relevant.

This is where the laser light shows and the M&M-tossing facilitators get it wrong. Both of these actions appeal to our sense of play, but neither gives the message that something of critical importance is onstage. Ask yourself, What does my audience most respect?

I created a Touchstone Event to open a knowledge-sharing event for the most senior project managers at NASA—those who have led programs that span decades. My program was about *balance.* Balance is critical to (1) satellite and probe operation, (2) large-scale project success (some of their projects have close to 100,000 individuals contributing), and (3) sustainability over the life of a twenty- to thirty-year program. Balance is easily symbolized by sculpture, so choosing dramatic visual representatives to catch their attention was easy.

Give the Head Something to Ponder

The mind is like a monkey: everywhere distracted and always looking for how to disrupt what is happening. This is why people jump to cynicism or poke fun at unusual activity as a first response. To clear this obstacle, give real data that provide genuine value and are fully integrated with your message. For NASA, we immediately involved the project managers in identifying the biggest challenge they faced. They provided their own data, and we got their minds involved.

Deliver the Heart

When addressing professionals, talk about what they love. Another way of saying this is get into what they care most about. For engineers, it is their most difficult and challenging problems. For researchers, it is their hot topics. For project managers, it is delivering on time under budget. For scientists, it is the frontier of knowledge. For salespeople, it is bringing in deals. You get the idea.

Catching People When They Are Ripe

In 2002 I was designated a Visionary by the Center for Association Leadership for my work with storytelling, community, and knowledge management. I spent that year collaborating with their senior staff and hundreds of association executives. Our primary focus together was how to build and leverage communities that would generate returns for the organizations that invested in them.

Meetings are a major component of most associations' business models and a significant service to members. Some associations (the American College of Cardiology is one of them) hold a very large annual meeting of around twenty-five thousand people. Others, like the International Bridge, Tunnel and Turnpike Association, spread their meetings out across the year, holding six to eight in a cycle.

Revenues are generated through registrations for many of these associations. For others, the meetings make possible other activities that generate significant portions of their revenue. For the Institute of Operations Research and the Management Sciences, the meetings make possible thousands of presentations that turn into papers submitted for publication in its twelve scholarly journals. Subscriptions to these journals are a major source of revenue.

The point is that associations take meetings seriously. For a year I worked with associations to pull apart and put meetings back together again, looking for opportunities to harvest the value they represent. One of the biggest opportunities we found happened *after the meeting was over,* in fact, just after it ended. Most organizations miss the boat here. It's all about catching people when they're ripe.

When a really important meeting is created, usually a team of people is responsible for all aspects of production—everything from marketing to registration to programming. Their work climbs an almost asymptotic curve as the date of the meeting approaches, with more and more effort expended the closer they get.

Finally, when the event occurs, they blow out, pouring all their available energy into creating success. Some of the most critical staffers live on caffeine and sleep three hours per night, handling all manner of unpredictable circumstances—everything from last-minute hotel changes to participants' personal crises.

When the event is over, everybody on staff crashes. In some organizations the team takes time off to catch up on sleep. The dark line in Figure 6.1 represents the energy of staff members relative to date of the event.

But the participants go through something quite different. Many of them do not think much about or put in much effort prior to the event other than travel. Then they come to the event, where, if all goes

FIGURE 6.1 Staff Members' Energy Curve

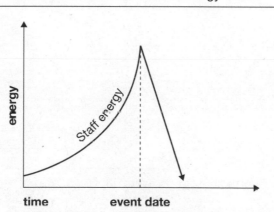

well, they become highly energized, motivated, and ready to act. As long as they are in each other's presence, they have a strong desire to take action, follow up on new ideas, reach out and build bridges, and implement what they have been talking about.

The critical junction happens not at the event, but just following it, as soon as the event is over and they leave. At this point, the rest of their life, held at bay during the event, returns. The e-mails and phone calls that piled up while they were away return. Requests for their input have escalated in urgency and demand. To maintain their enthusiasm, they need support, infusions of energy, and assistance. If they get it, they take off. If they don't, their commitment to the event's agenda plummets.

In Figure 6.2, you can see that the participants' energy has the potential to take off after the event *if* they get support. But without support, it drops precipitously. Just when the participants need support to act on what they have learned, the staff members are crashing. The result is that most meetings end up squandering their potential. In everyone's minds, it fades into the past as a memory of enthusiastic convergence, and not much more. This is what gives rise to the experience, "Oh, we never do anything other than talk."

FIGURE 6.2 Participants' Energy Curve

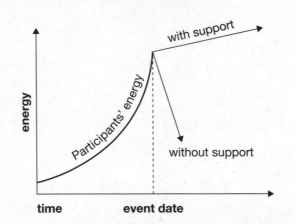

However, with a no more than a little help from a dedicated group of people, this same meeting has the potential to blossom. What you need is a second set of supporters who arrive at the meeting along with everyone else. They are on-site so they can watch the participants firsthand and understand their intentions. Then when the meeting is over, they are ready to provide support.

The support could be as simple as a phone call: "How are you doing? Did you have a chance to connect with Xavier? I saw a lot of interest in your idea, Have you spoken to anyone since we were together?" Or it could be more direct—for example, help with scheduling, providing contact, or resource information.

The point is if you want action to result, you need to catch people when they are ripe to execute. Yet the team that creates the event can get so wrapped up in their activity that they often miss the chance. Having a second team that goes in expressly to support the participants makes possible the value the event was designed to create.

FIVE WAYS TO SUPPORT PARTICIPANTS FOLLOWING A TOUCHSTONE EVENT

1. *Provide contact information.* Make it easy for everyone to get in touch with anyone who was present. Provide names, e-mail addresses, and telephone numbers at a minimum.
2. *Provide resources.* Create a bibliography of every book, paper, article, and Web site that was mentioned during the course of the gathering.
3. *Offer scheduling support.* Scheduling is one of the most time-consuming and frustrating activities to coordinate. Having someone on hand to offer assistance can make a big difference, helping participants to build their social network in order to carry out the intentions that will support your work.
4. *Nurture conversations and ideas.* Provide additional support materials that go beyond what was identified during the event. Do a little

research. Then send participants lists of additional publications, online resources, and names of people who can help develop the ideas that surfaced during the event.

5. *Provide collaborative technology where appropriate.* The general rule here is to serve a need rather than foist an application on an unreceptive audience. If people have a genuine need, provide them with an electronic list, a discussion forum, a Web site. You will know right away by the uptake if it's helpful. If so, get in and help it succeed.

The Single Most Powerful Way to Create a Dramatic Surge

This secret is well known in the entertainment industry. Imagine you are an agent, and one of your stars earns $3 million per night and you want to bump her up to $4 million a night. How do you do it? There really is no logical reason that someone should earn more than $3 million for a single performance, so you have to appeal to the emotions.

You do this by clustering her appearances and in the midst of the activity book your next set of engagements.

You work for a one-month period when your talent is in Las Vegas, New York, Chicago, Los Angeles, Dallas, and Minneapolis. During those same thirty days, you get her on the cover of every major magazine and on the air of every major talk show. It's a helluva month for the talent. She will be in nonstop peak performance mode for the entire thirty days. And she does this because the payoff is enormous.

Just before the big month starts, you begin reaching out to all of your contacts, telling them it is time to start planning ahead. As soon as the splash starts—that's what you call a densely coordinated set of events, a *splash*—you start cutting the next year's deals.

The people you are negotiating with notice that your talent is everywhere: on TV, the radio, in the press, playing all the big circuits. She must be packing the houses! They will think that surely she is worth the unreasonable amount of money you are charging.

The same principle works when you want to move a whole population of MVPs forward in a large, powerful rush. You create a splash. Here's how to do it:

Seven Steps to Staging Successful Splashes

1. *Get your timing right.* Begin contacting your partners and allies, and make sure the timing works for them. Check common calendars. You want to be the only game in town, so pick a slot that you can dominate.

2. *Build alliances.* Reach out to your major partners and MVPs, and explore how they can leverage your splash so that it generates win-wins across the board. These alliances will leverage your splash, amplifying its reach.

3. *Identify and work to your target audiences.* Know who you are trying to reach and the highest-leverage opportunities they present. Identify opportunities that can be clumped together in a short span of time.

4. *Prepare to execute.* Do rehearsals, and bring in administrative support to test everything in advance. When it gets to the go-live experience, you want as many of the kinks worked out in advance as possible. This is because you will be pouring energy into making each event a knockout and following up with people at the conclusion of each event. So in advance, take as much activity out of the execution as you can.

5. *Pull out all the stops on communication and marketing.* Make sure that everyone knows the full schedule of events. Leave no stone unturned. Contact people one-to-one. Visit groups to tell them firsthand what is coming. Get press to release information just before the events begin to take place. Get coverage during the sessions, and make sure it is reaching people.

6. *Prepare for exponential growth in participation.* Be ready for people who want to escalate their support as a result. Have staff members ready to support people.

7. *In the midst of activity, take decisive action on multiple fronts.* When your multi-event plan is in execution and people see evidence of your change program everywhere they look, engage them. Take advantage of the splash by moving aggressively and locking in a new set of commitments, moving things forward.

CREATING A SPLASH

Have a board presentation for senior staff the same week as an all-staff town hall and the dog-and-pony shows in the library. The following week, conduct a presentation at a high-profile project rollout, a sponsor's on-site visit, three divisional strategy sessions, and an all-staff Touchstone Event. Make sure everything about your event is friendly to your target audience's situation: timing, focus, and message. Sweat the small stuff. The more you can do to ensure 100 percent alignment among every component of your splash, the larger the burst will be.

Storytelling to Accelerate Growth

The American Nurses Credentialing Center (ANCC) has an annual conference that showcases magnet hospitals—those that have achieved magnet status by changing their culture to one that attracts and retains good nurses. In addition, they become centers of excellence in care. This means they have demonstrated lower patient mortality, greater collaboration between nurses and doctors, evidence-based data collection that drives innovation, and indicators that link to better financial performance.

In 2004 the ANCC came to me to deliver its conference keynote in Sacramento. Eighteen hundred nurses and other hospital professionals would be in the audience, and the ANCC was looking for an entertaining and informative presentation on the power of story.

In 2007 they again asked me to do a keynote, now looking for something wholly different. Almost five thousand people would be at this year's conference because the organization had been on a steep growth curve. This time they wanted the story to be about them and their success.

Together we designed a way to tell their story to the plenary. I interviewed over thirty people who had been involved with the ANCC in major ways: two of the researchers who started the program responsible for their dramatic growth, nurses, ANCC staff members, and hospital executives. I spoke with the past president and president of the board and other movers and shakers in the nursing profession. I interviewed CEOs who supported the magnet transformation.

From these conversations, I put together four components of the story:

- The history of the original research told by two of the researchers themselves
- The CEO's perspective
- The priorities delivered by the president
- The future of hospital excellence as seen by a recognized visionary

But the story was still incomplete. There were amazing chapters that came from among their attendees, like the hospital in Lebanon that had been operating inside a war zone for years and the breakthroughs in Australia where the hospital transformation had been successfully adapted to another health care culture. And we figured out how to include these in the storytelling.

I walked down off the stage during the plenary session and interviewed them like Oprah Winfrey venturing out into her audience. The cameras followed me, and we displayed them on the huge screens on either side of the stage.

And then there was the conference itself—an amazing explosion of spirit and celebration that brought nurses together with hospital executives to champion the cause. The conferences were truly remarkable, with great outpourings of devotion, ceremony, and splendid displays of pride and excitement. For example, when each of the previous year's magnet hospitals was announced, the representative nurses in the audience—usually eight to twelve people—would jump up screaming, blowing noisemakers, and throwing toys to everyone within reach. The teams worked hard to outdo each other. It was like a miniature carnival with everyone laughing and clapping in response.

I patrolled the hallways before my presentation with a video crew and created a three-minute man-on-the-street video that showcased all of the outrageous behavior, important events, international attendees, and large-scale activities like registration. This short video of highlights also became part of our onstage presentation.[2]

Finally, all the pieces were in place. These elements were combined into a storytelling extravaganza that told the story of the magnet program and the ANCC's dramatic growth, with video of thousands of participants. The presentation was videotaped.

The end result was more than a compelling video capture of an important piece of ANCC history. The video is an accelerator, helping the organization grow faster. It has an impact on their conference, informing and inspiring participants. I often return to produce a new, updated video, which they use as part of educational presentations describing the history of ANCC's growth, the magnet program, and the role of the conference in the organization's continued success.

This kind of storytelling is an effective tool to accelerate the growth of a movement.

EIGHT GUIDELINES FOR USING STORYTELLING TO ACCELERATE GROWTH

---

1. *Capture the history.* If possible, use the words of the people who were there.
2. *Provide data in a compelling narrative.* Use numbers to support the story, not the other way around.
3. *Tell the story through those who were there.* They convey the most authenticity and will provide treasured nuances that cannot be planned in advance.

4. *Give a strong picture of the present.* Lay out the challenges as well as the victories. Showcase the unique value being generated today.
5. *Point the way toward the future.* Bring in a visionary or two to show what is coming. Choose people who can rouse enthusiasm and inspire.
6. *Bring in the regular folk.* Showcase the ordinary people who carry out day-to-day operations.
7. *Highlight local heroes.* There are always exceptional stories to tell that feature everyday people making extraordinary contributions.
8. *Find ways to get everyone's picture into the story.* Work hard to include as many people as possible, one way or another.

Success Rules

- Touchstone Events dive deep and make contact with what is real, essential, and core in ways that generate dramatic sudden surges in forward momentum.
- Grabbing people's attention and keeping it requires reaching them through their gut, head, and heart.
- To make your event a success you have to be ready to catch people when they're ripe—just after the event.
- The single most powerful way to create a dramatic surge is by clustering events, creating a splash so that in a short span of time, your change initiative appears to be everywhere. Then, in the midst of this activity, you move forward on multiple fronts.
- Storytelling, done well, can move an entire community of MVPs forward.

7

Breaking Through Logjams

Ordinarily it is expedient to break a [log] jam as soon as possible. Once the river begins to fall, the logs settle and so press more firmly together. A very slight decrease in the volume of the water will lock the timber immovably.... If the jam happens to form between high banks, sooner or later the river will back up sufficiently behind it to flow over it. Naturally, when this happens, the logs on top are lifted, floated down, and precipitated over the breast of the jam into the stream below, where they either kill the men working at the breaking, or stick upright in the river bottom as a further obstruction. The formation of a jam, then, is a signal for feverish activity, and the man who is "driving" the river never breathes freely until his logs are once more racing down the current.

FRANK LESLIE'S POPULAR MONTHLY, JULY 1901[1]

The nineteenth-century logging industry in the United States reshaped the landscape, provided income for tens of thousands of workers, and was a significant source of economic resources in a difficult time.

In many wilderness areas, loggers would cut down trees, trim their branches and roots until they could be rolled easily, and haul them to the banks of a river. When spring floods came, the logs floated downstream to the mill on the current.

Imagine a rapidly flowing river packed with logs. Suddenly a change in course shifts the flow. Perhaps the width narrows, the channel jerks in a funny direction, or a group of boulders breaks the surface. The logs pile up amazingly fast, slamming into each other and backing up. The front of the jam locks down under severe pressure, forming a single, immovable mass.

Timber continues to pile in. The trees compress against each other with crushing strength, squeezing under the strain until they form a huge, tension-locked mass. The straining pressure is intensely dangerous. Water backs up behind them as if they were a dam, and the force cements them in place.

Crews of men set to work on them with all kinds of tools, from hand-axes to dynamite. It was dangerous work. Once the jam was broken, a torrent of heavy logs could rain down on the workers. Many men lost their lives clearing logjams.

The Great Log Jam of 1883 in Grand Rapids, Michigan, reportedly involved over 150 million feet of logs and was called one of the most terrific battles in the history of American industry. This was not just because the heroics of the men overcame tremendous odds stacked against them by physics. Their victory averted doom for the local economy. If the logjam had gone wrong, tremendous losses would have been incurred, including lumber valued in millions of dollars, the impact on the mills, thousands of jobs lost and as a result people losing their homes. In addition, the banks that held their notes would have collapsed, and there would have been domino consequences on local business.

The point of this story is to avoid getting into a logjam whenever possible. Nevertheless, they are an unavoidable part of change in a complex environment. Once they happen, break them as quickly as is safely possible to reduce the costs they can incur.

When a logjam occurs in your organization—that is, when the flow of positive change stops—get on it as soon as you can. Otherwise the organization begins to develop processes built on top of or around the difficulty, locking it into place. Other related activities then backfire, sometimes raining down on the very people working to get the change going again.

The Breakthrough Session

Notwithstanding the difficulties, logjams are a regular part of organizational life, as are obstacles of all other kinds: stalls, bottlenecks, derailments, miscommunication, and more.

So be prepared. Anticipate difficulties. Accept that they are part and parcel of successful implementation. Have a plan. When they occur, go to meet them. Use them as opportunities for a breakthrough.

Look at what causes an organizational logjam in the first place: Are leaders stymied? People stuck? Business processes colliding or broken? Tools cannot meet or keep up with challenges?

Dealing with logjams successfully reaps significant rewards: leaders on board, people busy executing, more effective business processes improving performance, the right tools for the challenges. It's hard work, often with high visibility and high risk. But the payoffs can be enormous. That is why I developed the Breakthrough Session, a template for bringing people together to iron out the toughest business issues.

The Breakthrough Session is for difficult and challenging problems that need multiple minds and representation from multiple points in the system to address. It is not a formula that generates a solution for a particular issue. Rather, it is a formula for engaging people successfully in the tough job of collaboration so they will work together to face difficult and challenging issues.

It is expensive. You have to bring people together and pay for their time. You may have to fly them in and put them up in a hotel. You or your team will spend a good deal of time doing the preparation and the follow-through. But if it's a breakthrough you're looking for, it's well worth it.

WHEN NOT TO DO A BREAKTHROUGH SESSION

- *The problem requires purely a technical fix.* People are working well together and ready to collaborate on implementing the solution, but the technology needs to be addressed.
- *The problem is not a priority.* Work can move along successfully without addressing it.
- *Ownership is clear, action is being taken, and results are forthcoming and timely.* Someone has the authority and is running with the issue. It's a matter of time before the issue is addressed, and there is no need to move it to the front burner.

In each of these instances, there is forward motion and no driving force calling the issue out to be addressed more immediately.

WHEN TO DO A BREAKTHROUGH SESSION

If you have problem that is critical or soon-to-be critical *and* one of the following conditions is met, you have cause for a Breakthrough Session:

- *It's a systemic problem.* Like smoothing out the covers on a bed, you get one area straight, but the wrinkles just travel to another location.
- *People have answers, but they're not getting together to work it out.* It's clear that certain individuals have what it takes to craft a solution, but you can't get everyone in the same place at the same time.
- *Authority is not clear.* The powers that be have been less than transparent on what needs to be done.
- *The obvious course keeps being avoided.* What needs to be done seems clear, but the organization keeps missing the mark.
- *No one owns the problem.* The issues has no home and as a result is not being addressed satisfactorily.
- *An energy drain in the system has formed.* People are losing enthusiasm for addressing a critical issue.

The Power of Face-to-Face

Breakthrough Sessions are not ordinary meetings. They are designed to rock the boat, breaking logjams. The time investment is significant, as well may be the financial investment. And these sessions rely on face-to-face engagement.

Face time is at a premium. It is difficult to make the time to travel to a common location for an extended period. What makes face-to-face engagement worth the effort are the three things you can get this way that you cannot get any other way:

- *Face-to-face is the ultimate trust-building medium.* People can build more robust trust in each other's presence. If trust is an issue, and it almost always is in a logjam, nothing beats face time for creating the rapport and firm belief in the reliability, truth, and ability of others.
- *Face-to-face speeds the resolution of complex issues.* When the situation consists of many different interrelated and connected parts, working together in the same place at the same time increases the pace at which solutions can be reached.
- *Face to face dramatically improves coordination in unpredictable environments.* Eyeball-to-eyeball beats voice-to-voice and screen-to-screen for increasing the ability of people to take a common understanding and implement it in situations that cannot be predicted. People who are shoulder-to-shoulder can convey and understand nuances that enable them to coordinate discrete activities across unpredictable circumstances.

Determining If Face-to-Face Is Required

To determine if face-to-face is required, look at the value the event can generate. Ask yourself these questions:

- What is the magnitude of our risk?
- Do we need a high-trust environment to generate solutions to critical issues?

- Are we facing complex issues that put us in jeopardy? Do we need to act consistently across multiple scenarios in ways that are hard to predict?
- What happens if we fail at this challenge?

If the answer is unbearable or unacceptable, the situation requires a face-to-face response.

You can also come at it from the other direction:

- What is the best possible outcome of bringing people together?
- What is that worth to the change program?
- How will we measure that impact?
- What are the costs and the offset?

If a face-to-face event will clearly generate substantial return, the answer is equally clear.

Anatomy of a Breakthrough Session

Once you have decided a Breakthrough Session is justified, you have a critical need on your hands. This is not an event to get wrong. Just as it has high potential for blowing through a bottleneck, it has the capacity to increase your difficulties.

The good news is that there are four things that will ensure your success, and each is within your control. By paying careful attention and staying alert, you won't make a misstep.

Four Requirements for a Successful Breakthrough

- *Be clear about your intent, and act accordingly.* Identify the central issue, and keep your eye on the ball. Everything is connected to everything else. As you speak to people and invite them to participate, the scope may appear to be expanding beyond reason. Keep your intent focused on the central activity.
- *Act in trust.* Success is predicated on the development of good relationships sustained by mutual support. Every interaction

should be seeded with the clear intent to do what is right and to ensure the safety and well-being of those involved. The individual bonds you maintain or establish will blossom into a feeling of pride, fellowship, and loyalty within the group. Once this is established, the breakthrough is practically assured.

- *Follow the steps.* Each of the steps outlined in the Six-Step Breakthrough Session Protocol later in this section contributes to a mounting momentum. The ultimate output of a successful Breakthrough Session is that the MVPs take the responsibilities for moving things forward themselves. To achieve this, you need to go each of the steps.

- *If circumstances change and they have a negative impact on the Breakthrough Session, stop.* Circumstances can change. If the situation shifts so that a Breakthrough Session is not needed, call off the session. Do not spend the political capital to bring people together and do the work required if it is not needed. Save it for when it is.

The Breakthrough Session is a special kind of meeting that brings people together to pool their know-how and experience, creating the collective intelligence and a common spirit of ingenuity to overcome the obstacles you are addressing and go beyond them to generate significant achievement. Every obstacle represents the opportunity to free up energy in the system. Rather than having it poured into a locking up of resources, it becomes free and available to carry out work. This is the ultimate goal.

In 2004 I began working with Gaddi Vasquez, director of the Peace Corps, and his thirty direct reports, all political appointees. Two challenges in particular were facing the group.

First, when the agency's mandate was created in 1961, its primary recruits were upper-middle-class white college graduates. By 2004 all that had changed. Their recruits now also included African Americans, Hispanics, and Asian Americans, as well as other ethnicities.

In addition, the age range had expanded to include retirees, and this meant that many had advanced degrees and significant professional experience.

Second, the Peace Corps was in the midst of designing an enterprise architecture that would revolutionize its business systems, bringing it into the twenty-first century.

Most of the senior staff did not understand the ramifications of these two major changes. In fact, the implications were complex and required significant study, as well as input from professionals with relevant expertise. The CIO, tasked with implementing the enterprise architecture, was concerned that the senior staff did not fully grasp the capabilities of the new technology. He was also an avid student of American demographics and wanted to increase appreciation among the senior team for the profound shifts the organization needed to undergo in order to adapt to its new clients.

After consultation with both Vasquez and the CIO, we agreed to adopt a breakthrough approach and followed the six steps I outline below. The retreat was held in 2005. The scope encompassed the shift in demographics and the new enterprise architecture. I interviewed all thirty people who attended. These conversations took thirty minutes per person, so I completed all interviews within two weeks easily.

In the first thirty minutes of the two-day event, I presented a summary of my findings. Short presentations addressing educational deficits highlighted demographic shifts and the implications for mission and marketing.

A series of stories had been created by the CIO and circulated that illustrated the changes the new enterprise architecture would bring to the organization. Most participants had read these stories, but it appeared there was still a large gap between their understanding and the new world that would soon be on them. And in a plenary discussion, several key people in high positions clearly did not fully support the new strategies the agency would be forced to adopt to stay relevant.

Prior to the retreat, the CIO and his team had developed a short theatrical piece that illustrated the dramatic changes the organization would be going through as a result of the new technology and new business processes and how they could be harnessed to meet the change in demographics. We had handed out the script and asked people to improvise. The spirit of play caught on, and people had a good time acting out the performance. There was a lot of laughter, and thanks to the good work of the CIO, several scenarios made their points dramatically.

The live skit demonstrated the power of the enterprise architecture in easy-to-imagine scenes from the organization's future. A palpable shift now took place among the senior staff as they saw the potential in the new technology. The authenticity of the moment, combined with the professional expertise of those present, overcame the previous challenges, and the group shifted into a high-performance state, generating energy and enthusiasm.

From that moment on, it was all we could do to keep up with the group's energy. They dropped the scripted agenda and gathered around a table to map out a way forward. Ideas were flying. The logjam had been cleared. Energy was released, and the senior team was performing at speeds beyond our predictions with greater collaboration among all parties.

To get to this point, I followed a six-step Breakthrough Session protocol outlined below. It was built as much on an admiration for the human spirit as it was on technical need. Every challenging conversation led us toward the eventual solution. Each step was critical in the overall achievement. The theater skit is not included in this protocol, but each situation demands its own brand of creativity to carry the day.

You will recognize many of the steps from previously in this book. That is because these techniques work in combination to produce remarkable results in a logjam.

The Six-Step Breakthrough Session Protocol

1. *Get the scope right.* Identify the area to address. This will determine what is relevant and what is not as you move forward, untangling interdependent relationships.

2. *Identify your Most Valuable Players.* Now you are looking at the group that is relevant to the logjam. Who needs to be in the room to find and initiate a real solution? This is your guest list.

3. *Conduct the interviews to map the territory.* Using the techniques in Chapter Four, contact people, and put together your Reconnaissance Report. Keep this in mind: because you are operating on a logjam, initial contact begins the process directing attention to the obstacle. Movement will begin immediately. There is a tendency to view this as preparation. In truth, the operation began with the first conversation.

4. *Set up the Breakthrough Session for success.* All bets ride on the outcome of the face-to-face event. Do everything in your power to ensure it is successful. Pour your heart and effort into establishing the conditions for success.

5. *Execution of the session itself.* Each step of the way, do everything you can do to press for results. This requires focused attention to the group's process. Your job is to ensure that the group takes up the challenge and deals with the issues as effectively as possible with a common intention to find the most productive way forward.

6. *Be ready to provide support in follow-up.* When the breakthrough occurs, it will require support to be carried out. Jump in and lend help where needed.

I have laid out these steps in general terms. The following sections crack open each of these steps to reveal in detail what is required to achieve dramatic results.

Getting Scope Right

Setting the proper scope is often more confusing than it seems. Ultimately it has to do with paying attention to the boundaries of time and impact. Initially scope seems pretty straightforward: you have a problem, and you want to fix it. But as you begin talking to people, you will find that two things happen.

First, the sense of what the issues are varies greatly from person to person. Each person will point you toward a locus of concern stemming from his or her point of view that is unique. The challenge is to decide which of the areas the various people toward should be part of the scope and which should not.

Second, you will find yourself zooming in and out like a microscope, focusing on both finer and coarser levels of granularity. Choosing the level that is appropriate can be a trial in itself.

To help you set your scope, turn first to time. How fast do you need a solution? This month? This quarter? This year? Identify the time envelope you need to operate inside, and refer to it when issues of scope challenge you. If you need a solution this month and someone asks you to consider expanding the scope to a set of issues not likely to be solved this year, make the decision to cap the scope so you reap the timely result you need.

Next, consider impact. What kind of impact are you looking for? In the example with Shell, Larry wanted to free up the energy in the system. He did not need to address innovation writ large or all technologies under consideration. He focused instead on the single application around which there was no forward movement.

Selecting Your MVPs

Chapter Three addressed choosing the select group of people who are capable of bring your initiative to life: your MVPs. Here we have a microcosm of that. This time it is the people who are authoring, enabling, and executing the significant and dramatic overcoming of an obstacle.

In this instance pay attention to four specialized categories:

- *Those who have the capacity to plan the breakthrough.* These are the people who have the knowledge and experience needed to design a real solution.
- *Representatives of those who will execute the breakthrough.* You need people present who know the coal face where the breakthrough will occur. These folks are familiar enough with day-to-day operations that they can raise both practical implementation issues and cultural barriers for examination.

- *Those required to enable the breakthrough.* Most successful innovations require a rewiring of business processes. This means money, time, and effort will be rerouted and business processes will be reengineered. You must have people in the room who have the political power to make these results happen.
- *Partners whose behavior will have to change.* Transformation has a point of high impact, as well as wider, peripheral repercussions. Many times there are critical partners who need to be involved in order to optimize the new way of working. For example, Forster brought in experts in the technology planning cycle. They were friendly to innovation and had to program resources well in advance of new technologies to ensure support was available. The technology folks had to adjust their planning process to contribute to our results.

Conducting the Interviews

As discussed in the Chapter Four, you will be conducting storylistening sessions and creating a Reconnaissance Report. For a breakthrough to occur, three important points require special consideration:

- *Provide a document as pre-reading that targets the scope.* Communicate to all parties the scope. Make it clear. Tell the story that illustrates the need for the breakthrough, and state the goal of the breakthrough cogently.
- *While keeping the scope stable, allow the list of MVPs to change.* Forster often referred to our roster of MVPs as a *dynamic* list because people were added and dropped throughout the process. Part of this was due to people coming and going in their job roles. Another part was due to absorbing new information as we conducted the interviews. In both cases, allowing the list of MVPs to adjust allowed us to hit the target.
- *See the invisible; imagine the impossible.* Logjams happen as a part of nature. Success takes a willing spirit to imagine innovation, successful transformation, and new business processes that do not yet exist. Do not be constrained by the ways things have

always been done or mind-sets invested in the status quo. In every interview, stay alert for the future that is emerging. I often ask, "What future does this seem to call out for that would require your participation to emerge?"

Setting the Session Up for Success

This is not a business-as-usual meeting. You must send the signal that a real breakthrough is taking place. Here are three ways to make that happen.

- *Get explicit endorsement from leaders.* Every breakthrough is different. Some require the president's signature, others the CIO's. Get them clearly involved, leaving no room for doubt as to their support. Perhaps even have them create a mandate. Sometimes this is best done in person. Bring them to the Breakthrough Session to speak or even participate when appropriate.
- *Make all relevant data available for inspection.* Gather together all information your participants may need, and have it on hand. This includes raw data, analysis, policies, strategy documents, and anything else that may be required to make progress.
- *Treat participants with respect.* You are asking people to come and give their best in redesigning the status quo and co-creating the future. Ultimately this is a voluntary act: you can mandate their participation but need their support. Communicate to them why they have been chosen, acknowledging their talent, experience, and expertise.

Execution of the Session Itself

Breakthrough Sessions are highly customized events shaped by the needs of the day. Nonetheless, there are guidelines for successful execution that apply across most applications. Here are fourteen principles to keep in mind:

1. *Lay out the room for optimum interaction.* Create an informal atmosphere. Arrange tables in a circle to make it easy for people to see the others present and look into each other's eyes as they

work together. Create an environment where people can get out of their chairs, refresh themselves, and stretch as needed, all without interrupting the flow of events. This is a roll-up-your-shirtsleeves-and-get-it-done session.

2. *Demonstrate the need for multiple points of view.* I use a ten-minute exercise where each person takes on the functional role of another in the room and describes the need for a breakthrough from that person's perspective. The goal is to value the others' perspectives and encourage complexity, both required for robust solutions to develop.

3. *Make participants' expertise explicit.* If you ask people to introduce themselves, most will not go into the special talents and relevant expertise they bring to the table. But this is critical information to get out in the open at the start. As the convener of the session, introduce each person, highlighting the skills and experience he or she brings to the session. You can do this quite effectively with less than a minute per person and quickly build an expectation of the group's high performance capacity.

4. *Accelerate rapport building through storytelling.* Storytelling is a critical skill for conveying context, enabling knowledge transfer from one situation to another. Jumpstart Storytelling is an excellent way to start a session that leverages each person's relevant experience and quickly builds the professional rapport required to engage effectively in difficult and complex issues. (See Appendix B for instructions.)

5. *Share the Reconnaissance Report.* This document lists everyone interviewed, which in a Breakthrough Session should include everyone in attendance. Hand this out at the beginning of the session and go over it together. When people see their name in print and hear their views accurately represented, most are instantly invested in the outcome. Furthermore, the collective views of the group are expressed through this document, which is valuable information for the participants.

6. *Address issues that matter most.* For this session to do its magic, no time must be wasted. This does not mean running participants

through a high-paced, no-time-to-think barrage of activities. Instead, treat the time as high-value opportunity. Prepare so that all materials are in place and the session can be devoted to the best possible use of time. Primarily this means addressing core issues, getting to the main points, and giving people the opportunity to change the way business is done.

7. *Provide the necessary educational components through succinct narrative presentations.* During the course of the interviews, it will become clear where education is required. For example, while working with Shell, we discovered that a missing piece for most of our MVPs was the knowledge of what it was like to operate the new technology in an operational setting. So we made contact with a team in Africa that had done it, and they created a presentation that was shared with the group.

8. *Identify and record issues as they emerge from the start.* As soon as issues are identified, record them using flip charts or a laptop and projector. However you record them, keep them visible in the room, which will accomplish three ends:

   • It will assure participants that they are being heard and give them a visible indicator that their issues are being recorded.

   • It will allow them to let go of searching for solutions until the appropriate time, which is critical to the event's flow.

   • It will capture them for use later while making it easier for participants to let go of addressing them immediately.

9. *Open the floor to discussion, and name all remaining issues.* Ask participants to identify all challenges and opportunities associated with the need for a breakthrough. Continue to capture them visibly, but do not seek to resolve them yet. Instead keep the conversation going, scouring the area for all relevant issues.

10. *Cluster the issues.* Once there is a sense that 80 to 90 percent of the issues have been identified, begin clustering them. You can keep adding issues as they arise. The purpose at this point is to begin to group interrelated issues into *nests,* associated clusters of issues

that have dependencies between them or are closely related in other ways. Name the cluster—for example, *regional impact, technical innovations, business processes to be reengineered, cultural challenges.*

11. *Assign nests to cross-functional teams within the group, and generate solutions.* Group participants by crossing job functions. Divide the number of nests so that each group has at least one. Have them work in small teams to generate solutions. Allow them to call others into their small teams as needed to consult with them. Each group prepares to report out by putting its presentation on a single flip-chart page. They must go to a high level of detail but still be able to represent all of their ideas on one page. If they insist, allow them two pages, but no more. The purpose is to force them to talk when it comes to finer levels of granularity. This is not a technical workout session; the focus is on the breakthrough, a higher-level issue. Once a course of action has been chosen, there will be time for technical workouts.

12. *Report out in plenary.* As each group identifies its solutions, allow others the time to ask clarifying questions. If specific solutions stand out as opportunities or first choice, identify them visibly (draw a star using a red marker, for example). Through discussion, the group will begin to hone in on its preferred breakthrough. Focus them on this. Challenge them with questions, ask for justification, and write down the decisions. Solution sets emerge as a result of the collective intelligence in the room that address multiple dimensions: culture, operations, policy, technical expertise, business drivers, and so on.

13. *Let participants lead.* As solutions begin to emerge during the plenary discussion, the energy in the room can rise considerably. At times, participants will take over. In the session at Shell, there came a point when they stopped following the script, grabbed a flip chart and laid it on a table, and then everyone stood around while the group identified the way forward. This kind of activity shows the group taking ownership of the solution—the ideal situation. Although it is sometimes difficult for the facilitator and convener to let go of the group process, it is an inflection point. The measure of success is the breakthrough itself. If it is being adequately

addressed, let the group lead. Intervene only to the extent required to ensure the breakthrough.

14. *Capture logistical requirements for effective follow-up and support.* Document all activities required for effective execution: the designation of responsibility, time lines, and dependencies. Share this along with contact information of all participants immediately following the session, and on the same day.

THREE REQUIREMENTS FOR THE EDUCATIONAL SESSIONS

1. *Ideally, have one of the MVPs present the material.* It will build the capacity and self-confidence of the group to have this knowledge in residence.

2. *Use first-person narrative, not PowerPoint, for the presentations.* People will tell you it can't be done, especially if they want to share technical knowledge. Nevertheless, give them a flip chart, and let them improvise. Tell them data sets can be used as supplemental handouts, but the presentation itself is to be done orally. For the breakthrough to occur, the emphasis must be on the people present. Make it personal, not abstract.

3. *Hold presentations to no more than ten minutes each.* People will cry, *Unreasonable! Can't be done!* Tell them to focus only on the most crucial points so that the material can be covered in ten minutes. In fact, the presentations will be longer. But the listeners will drive the content by their questions and discussion. You want the participants, not the presenter, to drive the granularity of the presentation. This is a way to guarantee that all the material presented will be relevant.

Providing Support in Follow-Up

Immediately following the session, and on the same day, provide participants with a rough outline of what took place—no more than a page in length. Include highlights and participants' contact information so they can carry forward as needed without waiting.

Within twenty-four hours, provide a more detailed account out-lining the designation of responsibility, time lines, and dependencies for follow-up activities, and copy this to relevant partners as a form of reporting out.

The Breakthrough Session is one of the highest-value interactions you will preside over. Treat it as a priority, and achieve excellence in carrying these out. You will find that logjams and obstacles are a regular part of change. Your ability to master addressing them will accelerate the speed of change dramatically.

LARRY FORSTER ON THE COMPETENCY FOR COLLABORATION

Expert Input

Larry Forster is a staff engineer with Shell Exploration and Production Company who works in technology planning and implementation in New Orleans. Having been involved in technology throughout his twenty-plus-year career in the oil and gas industry, he is a pioneer in engagement and collaboration.

Larry's use of story is mentioned in the book *Wake Me When the Data Is Over: How Organizations Use Stories to Drive Results.*[2] Larry has an amazing capacity to bring people together to deal with difficult issues firsthand.

When did you become interested in using collaboration as a way to create greater alignment among the people involved in your work?

It was late 2005. I learned there was a perception of misalignment between some of the people in my group and some of our partners in other parts of the organization. My role is a bridging role, and therefore, as soon as I heard there was even a slight sense of misalignment, I knew this was something that I owned.

How did you handle it?

First, I identified our stakeholders. Then I made it a point to talk to these people. I knew I needed to hear from them. I wanted to do a workshop to bring about greater alignment, so I wanted to hear what they thought before I got too far down the road. The insights I gleaned from talking to them would help me design the workshop. I also wanted to be sure that I included everyone who needed to be involved to get the best result.

About a month before the workshop, I had a conversation with my boss and my VP. I told them what I had learned from these conversations. I remember asking, "Do we need to have a workshop? Can we just do this by e-mail?" My VP said, "We need to get everyone together. It's a good idea to get everyone together and hear all these views in the same room. We'll have time for discussion, so any areas of concern can be aired and cleared with everyone present."

We had two workshops. I arranged for the VP from the other group to keynote the first meeting, and my VP attended. For the second workshop, both VPs decided to attend the entire session. They came and did more than work the crowd. They worked together and created a mechanism for people to approach them, without any negative repercussions, following an organizational decision. In effect, they removed a communication barrier, making it possible for any relevant stakeholder to raise important issues.

Do you think this one set of workshops was all you needed, or is this type of engagement something that you are going to use again? When we are talking about alignment between work groups, we are talking about issues that impact safety and our organization's value generation—our two most important issues. Therefore, we need to develop the competency for collaboration. This is not a one-off thing. This is part of effective work on an ongoing basis.

Success Rules

- Logjams are an unavoidable part of change in a complex environment. Once they happen, break them as quickly as is safely possible to reduce the costs they can incur.
- The Breakthrough Session provides a template for bringing people together to address the toughest business issues. They rely on face-to-face engagement, an expensive but extremely high-return proposition.

- High-value and high-risk face-to-face Breakthrough Sessions require sensitive and careful operation.
- The Breakthrough Session has a carefully designed protocol that will ensure dramatic results.
- Setting the right scope is fundamental to success. Use your time and impact requirements to help you get it right.
- Selecting your MVPs for a Breakthrough Session requires focusing on the people who will design, make possible, and implement the breakthrough.
- Conducting interviews to understand the territory of the breakthrough requires that you effectively communicate the scope to all parties, maintain a dynamic list of MVPs, and imagine the future.
- Breakthrough Sessions go beyond business as usual. You need to send the right signals to the participants so they come with the expectation that they can help design a real breakthrough.
- Although every Breakthrough Session is unique, there are guidelines and principles to follow that will ensure success.
- Immediately following the session, on the same day, provide participants with a pertinent summary and all materials required for them to begin working together.

WorkLifeSuccess
in the Midst of Change

Throughout this book, I have been focusing on engagement and collaboration, providing techniques for bringing people together to co-create the future and drive buy-in. Counter to this and complementing it is the force of leadership. Every change stems from the insights, actions, and bold acts of an individual. That is who this book is written for: you, the change leader.

Change leaders require a customized approach to self-care. Your ability to pull it off has immediate and profound consequences for the quality of change leadership you provide. Your job is unique. In contrast to those carrying out predefined work, you put your efforts into shifting the status quo, arousing and inspiring peers, marshaling collective intelligence, and facilitating a coordinated response from disparate parties, all the while staying in touch with changing circumstances and shifting tactics to maintain strategy and achieve results. This requires a very effective form of self-care.

All change leaders I have worked with live and breathe their work. They think about it all the time, pulling together lessons from every aspect of their lives and applying them to help with moving things forward. This does not mean they give up the rest of their lives. This does not mean that their health suffers, their families never see them, their hearts are closed and their bodies exhausted, or they have no fun. In fact, among the best leaders, the opposite is true.

Strong change leaders sustain their vision and energy by improving their health, having fun, pouring their energy into other worthy causes, creating special interactions with their families, having deep relationships with their partners, pursuing spiritual development, and cultivating their energy so they can give their best. This is in fact what makes it possible for them to get change right, challenge after challenge, rising more than they are pushed down, and prevailing to see results achieved.

It's a tall order for anyone. Those who are at the growing edge of change know that it requires significant strength and even greater mental clarity. They dedicate themselves to achieve inner and outer energy and power so they can rise to meet the demands of their work.

I call this high-spirited, high-performance state *WorkLifeSuccess.* Success in work is integrally connected to success in all aspects of life. They are, in fact, indivisible. Enthusiastic, clear-minded, high-functioning people deliver inspired leadership. This chapter is dedicated to helping you achieve this state of pervasive flourishing so you can take on major change.

WorkLifeSuccess Is a Way of Being

The ability to be high functioning arises from having a mind-set that knows optimal performance is reliant on total health. Job No. 1 is to care for yourself, putting and keeping you in the best possible state to meet challenges and succeed. That said, your well-being is interrelated with the comfort, health, and happiness of those around you. People are fundamentally social creatures, and those we relate to profoundly influence us.

Here are thirteen perspectives that effective leaders use to shape their behavior and responses to situations. These viewpoints work together, creating approaches to life that generate WorkLifeSuccess:

Thirteen Viewpoints for Generating WorkLifeSuccess

1. *I care for myself in all situations,* optimizing every set of circumstances to achieve the best possible environment for my health and

well-being. I actively cultivate my physical, mental, and spiritual development.

2. *I care for others,* seeking the well-being of all I can assist. I see myself as part of a larger community.

3. *Nature is the foreground in which life is played out.* It is not a backdrop I learn by studying the patterns of nature and working in accord with them.

4. *I see my work as an extension of my life,* fully integrated with my well-being. I recognize that my joie de vivre is a priority that increases my capacity and effectiveness.

5. *I keep things in perspective.* I don't get bent out of shape by small things. I know what is negotiable and what is not. Almost everything is negotiable.

6. *I recognize the power of my closest relationships,* investing what is required to develop and keep them in balance, especially those of my inner circle.

7. *I participate in the joys and sorrows that are a natural part of life,* giving myself fully to my experience in all dimensions.

8. *I harvest learning from every experience and carry it with me,* applying it wherever it can have positive impact.

9. *I work for those things I believe in,* dedicating my life's energy to goals that sustain my spirit and call out my personal best.

10. *I know that solutions to challenging issues are often not obvious and can be effectively solved by wading into the complexities of the situation,* then emerging with resolutions that provide the best of all available options.

11. *I see the challenges of my world as a personal opportunity to shape the future* for the better. I am a force of nature.

12. *I recognize that my understanding of the world is made of mental models and do not confuse them with the world.* I am always learning and adjusting my mental models to grow with the experience, knowledge and wisdom I gather.

13. *I look at both the parts and the whole, recognizing that each fragment has its own integrity while at the same time everything is fundamentally connected.*

These thirteen perspectives, explored in more detail in the following section, create a powerful synergy, working together to grow a human being's leadership capacity in all realms of their life. The sum effect for those who achieve such a strong relationship to their own well-being, the people they interact with, and the world at large can be awesome.

Approaches for Generating WorkLifeSuccess

The suggestions that follow give more information on generating WorkLifeSuccess and some techniques for getting change right.

I care for myself in all situations, optimizing every set of circumstances to achieve the best possible environment for my health and well-being. I actively cultivate my physical, mental, and spiritual development.

This requires effort and commitment. But it's necessary. In order to marshal exceptional strength in crises, we must cultivate impressive abilities by deliberately raising the bar on day-to-day performance. The payoff for working daily to cultivate uncommon abilities is stunning and has a strong impact on all aspects of our performance, including work. The most common obstacle cited for not putting in the effort for physical, mental, and spiritual development is time. Consider this: full development increases both the quality of your actions and your ability to increase your efforts when required for exceptional circumstances. It is not a matter of if extraordinary circumstances will arise, but when they will. This is part of life. Be ready.

Yes, it is true that finding time to work out, read, take in cultural events, and devote yourself to spiritual pursuits is a challenge. But it is a challenge that returns much more than it requires of you.

THREE TECHNIQUES FOR REALIZING THE TIME YOU NEED

1. *Devote your attention to the question: How can I be more effective with less effort?* Dedicating yourself to this question will yield results

that change the way you live. For example, when we were cultivating communities for the World Bank's Knowledge Management initiative, we realized that we needed one person to support each thematic group but we had no resources. So we found an intern program at George Washington University that supplied a graduate student in the KM field for five hundred dollars per semester. We then convinced each thematic group to fund an intern and in short order had interns for almost every group. Then we needed someone to manage the interns, so asked another intern to do that. We leveraged our insight and intentions and reaped extraordinary effectiveness with relatively little effort on our part. Apply this question to every area of your life to find where you are spending too much time and rectify that.

2. *Become expert at customizing your experience to suit your needs.* For example, consider these possibilities if you work out every morning: learn which hotels have the facilities you need, develop routines that do not require equipment, manage the time required for your exercise, build a home gym. Apply the same approach to all your physical, mental and spiritual requirements.

3. *Trim the fat from your life.* Time is the one resource no one can give you more of, yet we all waste it. Identify the behaviors and routines with which you waste your time, and cut them without mercy.

I care for others, seeking the well-being of all I can assist. I see myself as part of a larger community.

As children we are dependent on our community, our parents, our other caregivers. When we needed help or were in danger, we depended on them to care for us. The transition from childhood to adulthood reverses those roles: we now become the providers of those who depend on us for their safety and well-being.

Adulthood requires another role: taking responsibility for the future. When we were youngsters, we had to learn how to survive and successfully develop. As adults, we take on ensuring the well-being of our larger community. It is this very drive that causes us to get change right and implement the innovations that will improve our world while being sensitive to changing circumstance.

But it stems from a deep, fundamental part of our being—from our primal nature. As it is cultivated, it yields great satisfaction that nourishes our soul and revitalizes our health. This is one of the ways we care for our spirit. In return, we are rejuvenated.

Nature is the foreground in which life is played out. It is not a backdrop I learn by studying the patterns of nature and working in accord with them.

The natural world provides timeless lessons in how the life force is cultivated and developed. Ask any gardener, hiker, sailor, or anyone else who regularly spends time in nature. Direct experience with nature provides a learning laboratory unlike any other. Experience your connection to the natural world, and you will be rewarded with both inner fulfillment and a plethora of lessons that can be applied to getting change right.

Four Ways to Learn from Nature

1. *Take an issue for a walk.* In some indigenous traditions, there is a ritual in which you carry an issue you are struggling with into the wilderness. It could be for a long walk or even a multiday sojourn. The purpose is to seek guidance from the great outdoors.
2. *Pick up a hobby that puts you in touch with nature's cycles.* Everywhere I go, I meet gardeners, and we always have lots to share about what we are learning in relation to leading change. We talk about the seasons, the soil, the life of plants, protecting our gardens from pests, cultivating the most beautiful flowers or tastiest vegetables, and so on. But gardening is not for everyone. How about astronomy, camping, skiing, fishing, weather watching, flower arranging, painting landscapes, drawing bodies, whale watching, walking and observing, horseback riding? The list is long.
3. *Share in the delights of others.* Even if you don't pick up a hobby yourself, someone you are close to is sure to have one. Ask about it.

Engage her in a conversation about how her interest has influenced her life. You might share with her a challenge you are facing and play a game where you use her interest as a metaphor for finding a solution. This is a great innovation exercise. Just as powerfully, it builds your relationship with this person.

4. *When you travel, take an interest in the landscape and environment.* Every location has its challenges and special qualities that influence the ways people live. When I go to Santa Clara, California, I marvel at the orange trees lining the city streets. Once when I was in town to deliver a keynote speech, I went for a long walk to clear my head before presenting. There were so many oranges; they were everywhere, falling from the trees! The oranges were a refreshing sight to someone coming from Washington, D.C., and they helped to clear my mind. Take in the local wine country, visit the strawberry fields, delight in great fields of flowers, or walk in a park. While there, see what you can learn and apply to your WorkLifeSuccess.

WHAT I LEARNED FROM TAKING AN ISSUE FOR A WALK

Once I was struggling with a client who was heavy-handed in his leadership. It seemed to me that he was creating resistance with his authoritarian approach and thereby alienating his MVPs. We had discussions, but they did not lead to any satisfactory changes. I took this issue with me on a long walk on the C&O Canal in Washington, D.C.

While strolling along, I saw aggressive plants coexisting with the other wildlife and noticed two things. First, all plants were driven by the same life force: the desire to thrive. Second, some of the more aggressive plants were wiping out the others, taking over their sun space.

I brought these observations back to my client and used them to jump-start a conversation about his intentions. It was a successful conversation that led him to reflect on his leadership style and results. He decided to change some of his behavior and back off a bit. Imagine if all interventions were that easy!

Nature had provided a fertile reflection tool.

I see my work as an extension of my life, fully integrated with my well-being. I recognize my joie de vivre is a priority that increases my capacity and effectiveness.

Every teacher recognizes the vast difference between an unengaged student and one who is on fire with learning. When enthusiasm catches hold, great things happen. The word *enthusiasm* comes from the Greek *enthous,* which means "possessed by a god, inspired." Making exuberant enjoyment of life a priority is unusual for most people, yet it at the center of profound effectiveness. Knowing what makes you tick and cultivating it has far-reaching, positive reverberations in all areas of performance.

This is great news! It means you have permission to travel to exotic locations, take up wine tasting, spend more time with your children, become a fly-fishing expert, visit quilting bees across the country, or whatever else turns your nut! Investing in your own joy builds your resistance to stress, revives you when your battery is low, puts spring in your step, and makes you a worthy adversary.

I keep things in perspective. I don't get bent out of shape by small things. I know what is negotiable and what is not.

Almost everything is negotiable. Stress, however, closes down the mind's creativity, narrowing options. It is a disease of the modern workplace according to the U.N. International Labour Organisation.[1]

Make a point of exercising perspective. Cultivate an attitude of simultaneous investment and detachment. Invest yourself in achieving results while being detached from the ordinary obstacles life serves up. Become an expert in dissipating frustration. Your day-to-day quality of life will thank you. Your heart will thank you. Your family will thank you. And, yes, your change leadership will be more effective.

FOUR WAYS TO DEFEAT STRESS

1. *Humor.* Find a way to laugh at yourself.
2. *Mental agility.* Become adept at shifting perspectives quickly.

3. *Flexibility.* Practice bending without breaking. Improve your ability to let insignificant and small annoyances go by.
4. *Willingness to negotiate.* Be ready, eager, and prepared to discuss and search for agreement.

Each of these is an effective strategy for lessening or removing stress altogether. The result is increased capacity to successfully navigate adversity.

I recognize the power of my closest relationships, investing what is required to develop and keep them in balance, especially those of my inner circle.

Our closest family and friends provide ballast when life's seas become stormy, improving our stability amid turbulence. This inner circle has more impact than many of us would like to believe. Family and friends provide a proving ground for relationship competence. Challenges you are facing here demonstrate the limitation of your interpersonal communication expertise. Use it as an opportunity to improve.

What I am proposing in this book is a relationship-centric model of change, one that is based on interactions under a variety of circumstances. This means that interpersonal skills play a major role.

Moreover, standing in good relation to your closest peers and family members provides an excellent foundation for taking risks in the work world. The converse is also true: when your most personal relationships are suffering, being bold at work becomes difficult. It behooves you to treat these relationships as a priority and then bring all you learn to bear on your change efforts.

I participate in the joys and sorrows that are a natural part of life, giving myself fully to my experience in all dimensions.

Joys and sorrows are not only a part of our personal lives; they are part of our professional ones as well. To the extent that you engage in these powerful and moving events, you deepen your experience and improve your connections to the people who go through them with you.

Our first large-scale event inside the World Bank was to com-
memorate the tragedy of 9/11. This anguishing passage brought our
community together in a time of great trial. Many months later, the Celebration of Cultures likewise galvanized our community. Both events
built bridges and fortified the Bank's ability to handle the stress of
change productively.

**I harvest learning from every experience and carry it with me, apply-
ing it wherever it can have positive impact.**

Powerful leaders decompartmentalize their lives, drawing on every
experience in their repertoire to advance their cause. They are expert at
applying knowledge that comes from such diverse experiences as raising
a family, growing up in their home city, appearing before the board, or
navigating the challenges of caring for the elderly. These people have a
passion for learning from every event and incorporating this constant
stream of growth into all aspects of their work.

WHAT I LEARNED FROM A COLLEAGUE AND HER YOUNG DAUGHTER

My work on change draws freely on my experience with street theater,
rites of passage, and storytelling. This began in the first change initiative
I was involved with at the World Bank. My colleague, Lesley Shneier, was
raising her daughter as a single mother at that time. She often brought
her to our meetings when we worked late at night. I remember her little
girl crawling around under the table when we met, untying my shoelaces.
Their unique bond contributed to our team. Mothering is, of course,
very nurturing. At the same time, it is not typically part of office culture.
Lesley and her daughter informed our work with wonderful experiences.
Their presence regularly reminded me of both the profound power of
motherhood and the sheer joy of childhood. Each of these influenced
my work directly. I began to see a good part of my job as cultivating
communities, nurturing engagement, and helping professionals to find
their joy.

I work for those things I believe in, dedicating my life's energy to goals that sustain my spirit and call out my personal best.

By dedicating time and energy to activities that sustain your spirit, you weave a fabric of life experience that is permeated with deep caring and attention to detail. This rubs off on all the projects you lead, including change work.

I have noticed that many visionary leaders devote themselves to causes that matter deeply and see it as a source of both energy and inspiration when the going is tough.

I know that solutions to challenging issues are often not obvious and can be effectively solved by wading into the complexities of the situation, then emerging with resolutions that provide the best of all available options.

I once worked closely with the director of a government research facility that was also a hospital. There were great difficulties among the staff and management, occasionally breaking into angry outbursts during work. The atmosphere was cold, stiff and uncooperative.

After investigating the issues, it became clear that the history was complex and stemmed from a long string of incidents on the job between staff members and their managers. The director invested several months in hearing all sides of the issues. He worked extra hours so he could spend time listening to his reports.

He convened special one-on-one sessions, small groups of staff with complaints, and brought the entire staff together on two occasions. He encouraged staff members to be honest and as a result often got an earful. Over the course of several months, there were many heart-to-heart meetings between the director and individuals. Before solutions emerged, the tone in the hallways began to shift for the better as people saw evidence of the director's honest intents.

Finally everyone who was involved put together a set of recommendations. After careful review, the director endorsed the vast majority, explaining his position on all points. Action was never reduced to a small, simple set. Rather, it involved a series of commitments on many fronts and engaging practically everyone except for the newest employees and interns.

As a result of airing most of the tensions, solutions were fashioned, and the result was a dramatic shift in warmth among the staff for the better. The director maintained confidence throughout that by patient listening and a willingness to take all issues to heart, he could change the culture of his organization. He succeeded.

Effective leaders resist the temptation to boil down solutions to a simple formula. Instead, they open themselves up to complexities with intent to find appropriate solutions that are responsive to real and existing tensions.

I see the challenges of my world as a personal opportunity to shape the future for the better. I am a force of nature.

Many people resign themselves to poor conditions, claiming this is *the way things are.* Not so with effective change leaders. They take on responsibility for influencing the future, wringing from existence a better world. They see themselves as active participants in the unfolding world.

John Kotter on the Greatest Positive Impact

Expert Input

Harvard Business School professor John Kotter is a world-class authority on change leadership, perhaps best known for his eight-step model for leading successful change. His vision is "Millions Leading, Billions Benefiting." His body of work, which provides extensive help to those who lead change, matches his farsighted, noble intentions. Each of his seventeen books makes substantive contributions to the field, with powerful stories from his exposure to hundreds of organizations illustrating his findings. I have relied on his stories, techniques, and insights, many times in my work.

Kotter's recent book, *A Sense of Urgency,* is a stimulating and thoughtful extension of his work.[2] It is filled with actionable and practical tools for creating the kind of productive urgency that contributes to successful change.

You appear to have a sense of urgency yourself.

There is no question that I've got a sense of urgency. I think in terms of thirty years, but I get up every morning to figure out what I can do today to push things along. I have big aspirations and I believe (a) they're possible, but (b) let's face it, you can drop dead tomorrow. So I play it both ways. The only way you're going to work on big aspirations is by taking a long view. But if you're going to be realistic about things, you might only have two days . . . so, use them!

Your book, *A Sense of Urgency,* is written for leaders in organizations. Yet several times you point out that maintaining urgency is good for the individual and the world too.

That is what I believe and what I have found. Some people feel they are being pressed to provide more leadership by their superiors. They are not convinced they can make much of a difference.

If you dig into what most people call urgency, it is a frenetic, energy-draining, meeting-to-meeting, taskforce-to-taskforce, activity-and-not-productivity behavior. It is not helping them at all. But it looks like a sense of urgency. It couldn't be more different. It is as radically different as complacency is from real urgency. Getting that clear in my own head was an important distinction.

My messages are (a) you can make a difference in your organization—more than you think sometimes—and (b) collective differences have a big impact on society. Sometimes even single individuals have this kind of impact. There is no question that the greatest positive impact from a person demonstrating leadership is on him or her.

I recognize that my understanding of the world is made of mental models and do not confuse them with the world. I am always learning and adjusting my mental models to grow with the experience, knowledge, and wisdom I gather.

Those who are constantly refining their understanding of the world, ready to have assumptions challenged and deal with the resulting fallout, live in a world of perpetual possibility. They inhabit a universe in which they can fashion breakthroughs rather than resign themselves to the acceptance of unattractive circumstances.

SEVEN QUESTIONS TO UNEARTH ASSUMPTIONS

1. What is fundamental about the way you see this situation?
2. What is your judgment predicated on?
3. What are other ways of looking at this situation that are just as valid from a different point of view?
4. How could another person come to a completely different conclusion?
5. How can you interpret these same circumstances and arrive at an opposing verdict?
6. How could this mean the very opposite of what you think it does?
7. Is there any way the essence of this situation can be interpreted differently?

I look at both the parts and the whole, recognizing that each fragment has its own integrity while at the same time everything is fundamentally connected.

Effective leaders have a remarkable capability to see both the parts of an issue and at the same time its unbroken wholeness, recognizing the interconnectedness of all the pieces. This way of looking at the world makes it possible to see patterns that are nonlinear and complex.

For example, look at a set of the parts of a body: brain, heart, lungs, and skin. You see that each has a particular set of purposes, a unique and recognizable shape, and a special location. It is similar with the parts of an organization: accounting, operations, marketing, and so on. There is a real sense of identity to each component. It is, for example, fairly easy to recognize the lungs by their shape, and we can talk in general terms about their primary function.

At the same time, there is a great deal that each of these parts shares. They are all organs. Each must belong to a body in order to carry out that function. Each requires the others' activity to perform. The relationship between the brain and the skin is complex and not accurately conveyed through one-way cause and effect. In this sense it is nonlinear.

By seeing the organs—or parts of an organization—as both self-contained and interdependent, it is possible to have an appreciation for optimizing their collective performance as well as their individual functioning.

Clarity of Purpose

We all have ups and downs. When you are leading change, you learn how to manage your inner state to effectively provide leadership when the inevitable challenges arise. Amid changing circumstances, clarity is knowing what to do when, which directions to pursue, and how. As situations shift, so does context. What is right to do in one context can be inappropriate in another.

There are times when it is most helpful to be authoritative and forceful and to issue commands. At other times, a better choice of action is to be receptive and inviting, thereby encouraging collaboration. The behavior changes dramatically to fit the circumstance, yet the intent remains the same: to advance change.

Clarity of purpose and the wherewithal to continue in the face of opposition are the most precious resources a leader has. These attributes are at the foundation of WorkLifeSuccess as well.

When I say that the frontier of every transformation is in the minds of its leaders, I am referring to the agency we summon from within that motivates us to act and gives shape to our intentions.

How can you achieve clarity and arrive at the course of action that is most useful and appropriate? A technique that is quite helpful is using conscious dissonance to increase clarity.

Dissonance results from the coexistence of two or more elements that are out of harmony with each other. By paying attention to them, you can facilitate solutions that increase clarity.

Conscious dissonance refers to intentionally creating this lack of harmony by articulating current conditions and the goal you are seeking, allowing the tension between the two to be felt. Robert Fritz, the composer and filmmaker, calls this *structural tension* and says it is the structure of the creative process.[3]

The process goes like this:

1. Clearly articulate existing conditions, especially those aspects that are lacking, debilitating, or ultimately incompatible with your objectives.
2. Lay out in detail your objectives—the goals you want to realize.
3. Allow the two to sit side-by-side in your mind, emphasizing where they are out of sync with each other. This will create the conscious dissonance, or structural tension, that seeks resolution.

By focusing on dissonance, you create clarity. By highlighting differences between where you are and where you want to be, you find paths for getting from here to there. Those that fit the constraints you operate within and provide the best solutions will increase your clarity about what action to take. Effective leaders practice holding opposing images in their minds simultaneously, refusing to compromise on any one. Rather than choosing one or the other, they find ways for both to exist.

Roger Martin calls this *integrative thinking,* saying that this talent allows leaders to "embrace complexity, tolerate uncertainty, and manage tension in searching for creative solutions to problems."[4] All of these increase clarity.

The Power of an Outside Advisor

Leading change is demanding, requiring that you juggle an overwhelming number of balls simultaneously. It is easy to get out of balance, drop a ball, or become distracted by a crisis. One of the most effective ways that change leaders compensate is by bringing in an outside expert—an advisor with extensive experience who can provide solutions other leaders have used successfully and help you with strategic reflection.

Six Benefits of an Outside Advisor

1. *Input from similar experiences.* An experienced practitioner can draw on relevant experiences from other organizations, providing you with solutions to difficult challenges in short order.

2. *Professional support for situations you would otherwise face alone.* Leading can be a lonely job. Confidentiality can sometimes be so pervasive that it is necessary to make decisions without consulting anyone inside the organization. The outside advisor can provide support and a second opinion without breaking confidentiality.

3. *Confidence in the most difficult situations.* An experienced practitioner can provide you with information from relevant resources, including putting you in touch with others who have faced similar challenges and experts who provide knowledgeable guidance.

4. *A balanced perspective.* Sometimes it is important to get another perspective to balance the guidance you are receiving. One of my clients was responsible for a multimillion-dollar change program and hired a large consulting firm to put together the change management project plan. When it was completed, he gave it to me to review. The plan was a PowerPoint deck with over two hundred slides! It included everything you can imagine. Two points immediately surfaced. (1) Nothing rose to the top; there were no priorities established. Everything had equal weight. Because so many activities were described, it was difficult to know where to place emphasis, where we could get the most impact. (2) Engagement was weak. Statements like, "Get buy-in" and "Hold meetings to create support," were included with no additional detail. I met with the lead from the consulting firm, provided the feedback, and the plan was adjusted.

5. *Strategic reflection.* This is perhaps one of the most valuable services an advisor can provide: the opportunity to think together, sound out ideas, give voice to concerns in a safe environment. This opportunity directly improves your ability to digest information and experience, integrate disruptions and breakthroughs, and respond in the best way possible. Strategic reflection is exceptional. It provides the opportunity to examine assumptions, plans, and issues in relation to long-term aims and the means to achieve them. When it is done properly, misaligned activities and ideas become abundantly clear, as do those that can bolster or accelerate progress. The result is action that significantly advances your efforts.

6. *Feedback on warning signs of exhaustion or narrowing of response.* Many leaders push themselves hard and need assistance knowing when to slow down or take a break. It can be difficult to make that judgment call on your own, but an outside advisor can quickly point to the need for rejuvenation. "Time to take a nap!" or "Go on vacation!" is sometimes the best advice for an overworked leader.

Success Rules

- High-performance leaders integrate a successful approach to work and life, which I have termed *WorkLifeSuccess.* They see the world in unique ways that give rise to a powerful framework for getting results and satisfaction on all fronts.
- Time is a particular challenge, yet those who excel have found ways to work successfully with it.
- Nature is the original teacher, providing insights for how the natural order can be used to craft solutions.
- Stress is a killer. Exemplary leaders make a point of alleviating it.
- Questioning assumptions keeps our minds agile and flexible, maintaining the openness required for innovation.

- By intentionally highlighting the discord between current conditions and your goals, you create the structural tension that leads to solutions.
- One of the most effective ways change leaders support themselves is by bringing in an outside expert—an advisor with extensive experience who can provide solutions and strategic reflection.

Appendix A

Sample Strategic Engagement Plan

Overview

1. Our business processes are in the midst of a fundamental change. We are transforming our relationships, business processes, systems, and applications to provide more and better-quality products and services that improve our customers' conditions while increasing our revenues by more than 22 percent.

2. This will have a pervasive and systematic impact on the day-to-day work practices of all our employees around the world, so it is essential that staff be well informed, prepared to act, and engaged in our success. Their understanding is instrumental to:

a. Both the institutional and individual benefits and requirements, short and long term, of the overall change, as well as its specific components

b. The role our program plays in the organization's strategic objectives

c. How these changes will affect their jobs and work processes

d. What actions they can offer in order to be prepared and to master the new business processes.

3. This plan builds on activities already being carried out by the Senior Leadership Team (SLT) and the departments of Communications, Training, and Support. These include

a. Full integration with our Strategic Plan and Business Plan
b. The newsletter and periodicals
c. Meetings between the Change Leader's office and the Regional Leadership Teams
d. The Web site
e. Regular exhibits in our hallways and atriums
f. Skill and competency-based training programs at all levels
g. All Help Desk and Support activities

Role and Function of the Engagement Team

The principal role of the Engagement Team is to create enthusiastic support among all employees and external stakeholders through involving them in two-way conversations that educate about the change initiative as well as winning buy-in. Like all other team efforts, our effectiveness will be linked with that of all other major players in our strategic initiatives. We expect to collaborate closely with them in executing this program.

As engagement specialists, we will, in consultation with our principal clients, develop umbrella activities that will make it easy and interesting for staff to move from awareness to understanding, engagement, contribution, and fluent use as co-creators in our success. We will provide support services to ensure widespread accessibility of the essential information that this program conveys and provide presentation training and support as requested. However, all substantive information related to specific business impacts will be developed by the business content experts.

As strategic event planners, we will make recommendations, provide support materials and human resources, and make the logistical arrangements when requested to support briefings, town halls, video-conferences, and other special events. We will promote them through appropriate media, working closely with the Communications team to ensure full integration with all other strategic initiatives.

As promoters, we will work with the External Relations department to ensure that our interactions with external stakeholders are fully integrated with all other efforts.

Conditions for Success

Active Leadership and Quick Decisions

The success of this initiative will depend on a precise methodology for communications clearance, providing approval to act quickly when necessary.

The Approval Process

For the fundamental engagement activities, including this action plan, sign-off will be given by the group reviewing this plan: the CEO, CFO, COO, CIO and CMO.

Subsequently, the leads for change will be responsible for sign-off.

All requests for sign-off will be copied to the representative of the Senior Leadership Team. They will have twenty-four hours in which to raise issues for consideration. However, final decisions rest with the COO.

Committed Participation from the Change Leadership Team and Line Managers

Our training experts stress that staff members respond best to action messages that are delivered directly by their immediate supervisors. Everyone needs training, and training will be more effective if trainees arrive with the proper advance preparation. This makes the role of the line manager critical to the success of the launch.

The Change Leadership Team members are our main point of access to line managers and downstream staff. Therefore, much of the campaign's success hangs on their effectiveness. We must communicate with them directly, participate actively in their joint planning meetings, and brief them on the purpose and use of engagement materials. We will provide a significant amount of encouragement and recognition throughout the campaign and draw on the SLT for this regularly.

Adequate Investment

This program is a huge financial and philosophical investment. Even more important, it will require a major change in mind-set because it will change the way everyone works. This kind of unprecedented change agency requires an investment from each individual commensurate with that of the company.

Experience has shown that an investment equal to 1 to 3 percent of the total change investment should be considered the minimum to forestall the need for expenditure in crisis communications later.

Strategic Foundations for Engagement

1. *Timeliness.* From the engagement perspective, launching this program and its related business integration processes is a time-sensitive campaign. Our campaign will build toward the launch date. We will highlight milestones to prepare all participants to take the appropriate actions that lead up to the transformation and assist them in adjusting to the changes by providing relevant information in the days immediately following introduction.

2. *A strong theme and clear message.* The complexity of the overall initiative and the compressed time schedule demand that we work within a memorable umbrella theme with consistent, focused messages and back them with strong graphics, marketing materials, and events that will carry through all communication efforts, regardless of target audience. The engagement team will work in lockstep with communications.

3. *Credibility.* In our campaign, we must tell the truth about the benefits as well as prepare staff to meet the inevitable frustrations inherent in making a change of this magnitude. We must also demonstrate our ability to act as an effective listening tool for the entire change program. Two-way conversation will be our modus operandi, demonstrating authentic collaboration as our primary way forward.

4. *Value.* All engagements will be linked to clear value for participants, the change program, the organization as a whole, and the world at large. It is our honest intention to create better circumstances and improve performance for every system we are a member of.

5. *Respect and inquiry.* Engagement is an act of inquiry and thrives on new perspectives and insights. In all our work, we will endeavor to understand differing points of view and effectively integrate them so as to maximize the value we generate. We will explicitly seek out alternate points of view and consciously choose whether to integrate them going forward.

Objectives: Service to Staff and Management

This engagement campaign has five interrelated objectives:

1. *Generate awareness* of the impending changes as well as the need for and availability of training.
2. *Build initial understanding* of the challenges and opportunities.
3. *Promote action* to enroll staff and act on alternate points of view.
4. *Enhance understanding* through interactive dialogue during all phases of implementation.
5. *Build commitment* among managers and end-users as implementation progresses.

Appendix B

JumpStart Storytelling

Imagine a two-day think-tank of business professionals coming together to address critical issues. The first session is the toughest because everyone brings their competing views to the table and kicks off the event with a prove-it-to-me attitude that says, "Show me what you can do for me."

That's the kind of event that I have been asked to lead over and again. And each time I have used Jumpstart Storytelling to propel the retreat into a high performance collaboration event, drawing everyone together and highlighting the diversity of perspectives without pushing for consensus. This process lifts the collective spirit and maximizes the impact of people's time together. It quickly engages participants in the business at hand and accelerates productive work.

Designed for groups of 10–100, I have customized it for as few as three and as many as 2,500. It takes 45–60 minutes regardless of the

Excerpted from S. Kahan, "The Power of Storytelling to JumpStart Collaboration," *Journal for Quality and Participation*, Spring 2006, pp. 24–25. Reprinted with permission from *Journal for Quality and Participation*, © 2006 American Society for Quality.

number of people, creating an esprit de corps that sets the stage for high-performance collaboration.

I designed JumpStart Storytelling based on my work at the World Bank, where it was field tested on multicultural gatherings more than 100 times. It also draws on techniques I learned from Paul Costello while on a fellowship at the Center for Narrative Studies,[1] and working as a designated "Visionary" for the Center for Association Leadership to increase the effectiveness of professional meetings and conventions.

The purposes of JumpStart Storytelling include

- Efficiently engaging every participant in the business objectives.
- Accelerating collaboration without compromising diverse perspectives.
- Effectively introducing each person to 10–15 other participants.
- Improve learning through high quality idea exchange.

Here's how I run a session of JumpStart Storytelling:

1. I put people in groups of 6–8 and ask them to think of a story that has to do with the primary business objectives of the meeting, drawn from their own experience. For example, at a recent meeting of CEOs facing the prospects of competing with China, I asked them to tell a story about a time in their lives when they faced a daunting challenge that changed the way they see the world.

I ask them to tell their story to the other members at the table, in just 90 seconds. So, they only have time to relay the essence of their experience. I encourage them to give enough background to explain why the challenge was daunting, how they met it, and how their worldview changed. In other words, without saying as much, I encouraged them to tell the arc of their personal story.

I keep time, letting him or her know when each person has 30 seconds left, and then calling for the next person after 90 seconds. "However," I tell the participants, "while it may be my job to get the whole room through the process in nine minutes (for tables of six), it's not your job.

So, if your story is a little long, go with it. And if your story is over in less time, move on to the next person."

I am encouraging each group to self-manage their time so they get the spirit that they are in charge of their experience. This is an important element, setting the stage for the ownership effective collaboration requires.

When the first round of stories is done, I ask them to look around the table and bring to mind the story that most impacted them, and remember the teller.

2. I get everyone up out of his or her chair and find a new table with mostly new faces; it's time for the second round. People are to tell the same story they told in the first round.

In U.S. audiences I typically hear groans at this point because we seem to be uncomfortable with repeating ourselves. I make light of the situation, explaining that in other cultures people enjoy telling their stories over and over; it's a way of life.

I ask people to notice what changes and what stays the same when they tell their story a second time, and how interesting it is that the words are different, but the story is the same. I use the same process as in the first round, moving people through in 90-second intervals.

3. Now for the real fun. I ask everyone in the room to recall the story that most impacted them, either because they found it moving or because the information it contained was so relevant to today's gathering. Then, they are to get out of their seat and find the person who told that story. When they find the storyteller they are to put their hand on the person's shoulder and keep it there.

What happens next is remarkable: a live demonstration of social networking that I call "clusters and chains." The room appears to go into chaos as people search for others and move around the room with trailing chains and clusters of people attached to them. In short order, no matter the number of participants, this process sorts itself out.

The room is literally a configuration of clusters and chains, with those tellers who made the most impact with the most hands on their shoulders.

4. I ask for those with the most hands on their shoulders to come to the front of the room and tell their stories to the plenary. The participants, not the conveners or the facilitator, selected these stories. We spend some time together unpacking these stories and discovering why they were chosen.

The magic of Jumpstart Storytelling occurs when participants tell and listen to each other's stories, engaging the hearts and minds of their colleagues.

It is a great way to begin a business gathering, involving everyone in the room. Ideas cross-pollinate and rapport increases. The entire meeting comes to life in a way that naturally and predictably focuses the audience's collective enthusiasm on the business at hand through the participants' personal stories.

Storytelling is part of human experience. When people share their stories, listeners naturally focus their attention, engaging with the teller's experience. The deliberate and effective use of storytelling establishes links between participants, and sets the stage for high performance.

To create an atmosphere of collaboration it is necessary to shift away from a "broadcast" mode in which one person speaks while everyone else listens. By activating a "beehive"[2] in which everyone is sharing, the conversation moves off the podium and out onto the floor. This form of storytelling has the effect of filling the room with relevant activity and enthusiasm.

Social networking is one of the primary reasons people attend professional gatherings. Many transactions take place in the hallways: valuable news is exchanged, services and jobs are brokered, new members are integrated within existing communities or not.

The capacity for each person to build and develop relationships during the meeting increases as they are informally introduced to others and invited to share their stories in the context of business. This sharing is personal and face-to-face, providing a rich interaction, which significantly increases the capacity of the group for social networking.

High quality collaboration relies on multiple, conflicting points of view coming together in a collective intelligence that honors the contribution of each perspective. Building community is often mistakenly thought of as creating an environment where everybody likes each other. People perform effectively without mutual admiration. Yet, it is critical to establish an atmosphere of collective aspiration built upon respect and the capacity for each person to contribute to the group's objectives. Storytelling brings together differing points of view in the spirit of collaboration.

Notes

Chapter One

1   Weaver, W., and Shannon, C. E. *The Mathematical Theory of Communication.* Urbana: University of Illinois Press, 1949.

2   Hollnagel, E., and Woods, D. D. *Joint Cognitive Systems: Foundations of Cognitive Systems Engineering.* Boca Raton, Fla.: CRC Press, 2005.

3   Heckelman, J. "Constructing Ken Gergen: The Maverick Psychologist Continues to Reinvent a Shifting Self." *Swarthmore College Bulletin,* June 2002.

4   Denning, S. *The Leader's Guide to Storytelling.* San Francisco: Jossey-Bass, 2005. Denning, S. *The Secret Language of Leadership.* San Francisco: Jossey-Bass, 2007.

5   Stern, S. "Review of S. Denning, *The Secret Language of Leadership.*" *Financial Times,* Aug. 29, 2007.

Chapter Two

1   Denning, S. *The Springboard: How Storytelling Ignites Action in Knowledge-Era Organizations.* Burlington, Mass.: Butterworth Heinemann, 2001.

2 NAPPS evolved into two groups: the National Storytelling Network, dedicated to advancing the art of storytelling by providing resources to storytellers and event planners (http://www.storynet.org), and the International Storytelling Center, promoting the power of storytelling and its creative applications to build a better world (http://www .storytellingcenter.net).

3 Denning. *The Springboard.*

4 Heifetz, R., and Linsky, M. *Leadership on the Line: Staying Alive Through the Dangers of Leading.* Boston: Harvard Business School Press, 2002.

Chapter Four

1 Blair, M. *Riding the Current: True Stories and Tested Techniques for Keeping Your Knowledge Fresh and Your Work Alive.* Chagrin Falls, Ohio: Taos Institute, 2009.

Chapter Five

1 Wenger, E. *Communities of Practice: Learning, Meaning, and Identity.* Cambridge: Cambridge University Press, 1998.

2 CPsquare (CP2) stands for the Community of Practice on Communities of Practice. According to its Web site (http://cpsquare.org), "CPsquare is like a town square, a place where people gather to connect and learn together. We are from corporate, private, non-profit, and academic organizations; we hail from many nations across the globe; we are involved in consulting, research, and direct support of communities of practice; and we join together to create our own community of practice."

3 Wenger, E. "Learning for a Small Planet: A Research Agenda." Sept. 2006, available at http://www.ewenger.com.

4 Ibid., p. 21.

5 Wenger, E., McDermott, R., and Snyder, William M. *Cultivating Communities of Practice.* Boston: Harvard Business School Press, 2002.

6 Lave, J., and Wenger, E., *Situated Learning: Legitimate Peripheral Participation.* Cambridge: Cambridge University Press, 1991.

Chapter Six

1 For more information on rites of passage, read Arnold van Gennep (1873–1957), a noted French ethnographer (*Les rites de passage* originally published in 1909, reprinted as *The Rites of Passage* by the University of Chicago Press, 1961), anthropologist Victor Turner, who wrote two seminal works: *The Ritual Process: Structure and Anti-Structure* (originally published in 1969, reprinted by Aldine Transaction in 1995) and *From Ritual to Theatre: The Human Seriousness of Play* (PAJ Publications, 1982); and mythologist Joseph Campbell (*The Hero with a Thousand Faces*, Pantheon Press, 1949).

2 A copy of the three-minute video is on my Web site (VisionaryLeadership .com). The longer session is available as a DVD from the American Nurses Credentialing Center.

Chapter Seven

1 Frank Leslie (1821–1880) was an engraver and publisher of illustrated journals. He published *Frank Leslie's Popular Monthly* from 1876 to 1906, after which it became *American Magazine*. The article that this quotation is from, "The Great Logjam," by Stewart Edward White, can be found at http://www.catskillarchive.com/rrextra/lgjam.Html.

2 Silverman, L. (ed.). *Wake Me When the Data Is Over: How Organizations Use Stories to Drive Results.* San Francisco: Jossey-Bass, 2006.

Chapter Eight

1 Swoboda, F. "Employers Recognizing What Stress Costs Them, U.N. Report Suggests." *Washington Post,* Mar. 28, 1993.

2 Kotter, J. *A Sense of Urgency.* Boston: Harvard Business Press, 2008.

3 Fritz, R. *The Path of Least Resistance: Learning to Become the Creative Force in Your Own Life.* New York: Ballantine Books, 1989.

4 Martin, R. "The Art of Integrative Thinking." *Rotman Management,* Fall 1999, pp. 2–5.

Appendix B

1   The Center for Narrative Studies, run by Paul Costello, is a research and
    training institution (www.StoryWise.com).

2   This term is drawn from my booklet, *Building Beehives: A Handbook for
    Creating Communities That Generate Returns* (Bethesda, Md.: Performance
    Development Group, 2004).

Acknowledgments

There are four people I want like to single out for their contribution to my work.

My father, Robert Sydney Kahan, taught me by example what it means to be a great teacher. When I was in high school, I used to skip class and head over to his classroom at the University of Texas, where he would let me sit in on his graduate studies programs. Watching him in dialogue with his students, thinking together with them, inspires me to this day.

My wife, Laura Baron, provides me with unflinching support as I make my way clumsily toward that which most inspires me: my vocation. I remember waking one morning early in 2003, not quite a year after I left my job at the World Bank. I didn't have a single engagement at the time and awoke in anxiety. She brought the phone over to me, still in bed and in my pajamas, and told me to call a potential client right then. Ten minutes later, I had a contract worth fifty thousand dollars. She is my Polaris.

Steve Denning was my boss at the World Bank during the first large-scale change initiative I participated in. For two years, we worked side by side through the ups and downs that made milestones along our way. Today we often still have the chance to work side by side.

I remember one of our joint engagements, sharing the bill at a conference. We had been traveling quite a bit. I was sitting in the front row waiting my turn, while Steve was on stage addressing the crowd. He was clearly enjoying himself and meant to say so. His words came tumbling out: "It's good to be here in . . ." Then he looked down at me and said, "Seth, what city are we in?" I had to smile because it didn't really matter. The joy of being together with people who were eager to learn trumped all. (It was San Francisco.)

Every day my son, Gabriel, reminds me that the world will belong to his generation soon enough. My love for him is transcendent. He is the reason I persist, especially when I face challenges. He inspires me to go on trying to make the world a better place, helping visionaries everywhere to get change right.

About the Author

S eth Kahan is an international speaker, trainer, and consultant who has worked with CEOs and senior leaders responsible for large-scale change. His clients include Shell, the World Bank, Peace Corps, NASA, Marriott International, Project Management Institute, the American Public Transportation Association, the International Bridge Tunnel and Turnpike Association, the American Nurses Credentialing Center, HR Certification Institute, and Johns Hopkins University Applied Physics Laboratory.

He is the author of Fast Company's expert blog, *Leading Change* (SethFast.com), and a regular contributor to the *Washington Post* column, "On Success" (SethPost.com). Seth is an associate of the Taos Institute. He received the designation of Visionary by the Center for Association Leadership. The Society for the Advancement of Consulting has recognized him as a Thought-leader and Exemplar in the field of Change Leadership. You can learn more about his work by visiting him online at VisionaryLeadership.com.

Index